Pulling Strings with Puppet

Configuration Management Made Easy

JAMES TURNBULL

firstPress™

Pulling Strings with Puppet: Configuration Management Made Easy

Copyright © 2007 by James Turnbull

ISBN-13: 978-1-59059-978-5

ISBN-10: 1-59059-978-0

eISBN-13: 978-1-4302-0622-4

Printed and bound in the United States of America (POD)

Trademarked names may appear in this book. Rather than use a trademark symbol with every occurrence of a trademarked name, we use the names only in an editorial fashion and to the benefit of the trademark owner, with no intention of infringement of the trademark.

Java™ and all Java-based marks are trademarks or registered trademarks of Sun Microsystems, Inc., in the United States and other countries. Apress, Inc., is not affiliated with Sun Microsystems, Inc., and this book was written without endorsement from Sun Microsystems, Inc.

Lead Editors: Jason Gilmore, Joseph Ottinger

Technical Reviewer: Dennis Matotek

Editorial Board: Steve Anglin, Ewan Buckingham, Tony Campbell, Gary Cornell, Jonathan Gennick, Jason Gilmore, Kevin Goff, Jonathan Hassell, Matthew Moodie, Joseph Ottinger, Jeffrey Pepper, Ben Renow-Clarke, Dominic Shakeshaft, Matt Wade, Tom Welsh

Project Manager: Beth Christmas

Copy Editor: Ami Knox

Associate Production Director: Kari Brooks-Copony

Compositor: Richard Ables

Cover Designer: Kurt Krames

Manufacturing Director: Tom Debolski

Distributed to the book trade worldwide by Springer-Verlag New York, Inc., 233 Spring Street, 6th Floor, New York, NY 10013. Phone 1-800-SPRINGER, fax 201-348-4505, e-mail orders-ny@springer-sbm.com, or visit http://www.springeronline.com.

For information on translations, please contact Apress directly at 2855 Telegraph Avenue, Suite 600, Berkeley, CA 94705. Phone 510-549-5930, fax 510-549-5939, e-mail info@apress.com, or visit http://www.apress.com.

The information in this book is distributed on an "as is" basis, without warranty. Although every precaution has been taken in the preparation of this work, neither the author(s) nor Apress shall have any liability to any person or entity with respect to any loss or damage caused or alleged to be caused directly or indirectly by the information contained in this work.

The source code for this book is available to readers at http://www.apress.com in the Source Code/Download section.

This book is dedicated to Ruth Brown, who makes me laugh, and to my family for their continued support.

Contents

About the Author

JAMES TURNBULL works for the National Australia Bank as a Security Architect. He is the author of Hardening Linux, which focuses on hardening Linux hosts, and Pro Nagios 2.0, which focuses on enterprise management using the Nagios open source tool.

James has previously worked as an executive manager for IT security at the Commonwealth Bank of Australia, the CIO of a medical research foundation, manager of the architecture group of an outsourcing company, and in a number of IT roles in gaming, telecommunications, and government. He is an experienced infrastructure architect with a background in Linux/Unix, AS/400, Windows, and storage systems. He has been involved in security consulting, infrastructure security design, SLA, and service definition, and has an abiding interest in security metrics and measurement.

Acknowledgments

Luke Kanies—for writing Puppet and being kind enough to answer my numerous queries and questions.

The many members of the Puppet community who answered numerous questions and generally let me bother them.

Dennis Matotek for his technical review.

The team at Apress-Jason Gilmore, Joseph Ottinger, Beth Christmas, Ami Knox, Tina Nielsen, and Julie Miller-without all of you, none of this would be possible.

Jim Sumser for getting me started.

Introduction

This book introduces the reader to Puppet—a Ruby-based configuration management and automation tool for Linux and Unix platforms. The book is a beginning-to-intermediate guide to Puppet. It is aimed at system administrators, operators, systems engineers, and anyone else who has to manage Linux and Unix hosts.

This book requires a basic understanding of Linux/Unix systems administration including package management, user management, using a text editor such as vi, and some basic network and service management skills. If you wish to extend Puppet, you will need to have an understanding and some aptitude with the Ruby programming language. But for simple expansion of Puppet, basic Ruby skills are all that are needed. Additionally, as a programming language, Ruby is very approachable and easy to pick up.

The book starts with explaining how Puppet works and then moves on to installation and configuration. Each succeeding chapter introduces another facet of Puppet right up to demonstrating how you can extend Puppet yourself.

Chapter 1: Introduction to Puppet

Chapter 2: Installing and configuring Puppet

Chapter 3: Puppet's configuration language

Chapter 4: Using Puppet, which you learn through practical examples

Chapter 5: Reporting with Puppet

Chapter 6: Advanced Puppet features including integration with LDAP, performance management, and scalability

Chapter 7: Extending Puppet and Facter including adding your own Facter "facts" and Puppet configuration types

All of the source code, associated scripts, and configuration examples can be downloaded from the Apress web site. You can also submit any errata at the site.

If you have any questions and queries about the book, please do not hesitate to e-mail me at james@hardening-linux.com.

CHAPTER 1

Introducing Puppet

The lives of system administrators and in general individuals employed in IT's operational sector often revolve around a series of repetitive tasks: configuring hosts, creating users, and managing applications, daemons, and services. Often these tasks are repeated many times in the life cycle of one host in order to add new configuration or remedy configuration that has changed through error, entropy, or development. These tasks can be an ineffective use of time and effort.

The usual first response to these tasks is to try to automate them. This leads to the development of custom-built scripts and applications. In my first role as an administrator, I remember creating a collection of Control Language (CL) and Rexx scripts that I subsequently used to manage and operate a variety of infrastructure. Very little of the scripts developed in this ad hoc manner are ever published, documented, or reused. Indeed, copyright for most custom material rests with the operator or administrator's organization and is usually left behind when they move on. This leads to the same tool being developed over and over again.

Custom scripts and applications rarely scale to suit large environments and often have issues of stability, flexibility, and functionality. Such scripts also tend to suit only one target platform, resulting in situations such as the need to create a user creation script for BSD, one for Linux, and still another for Solaris. This increases the time and effort required to develop and maintain the very tools you are hoping to use to reduce administrative efforts.

Other approaches include the purchase of configuration management applications like Opsware, BMC's CONTROL-M, and CA's Unicenter products. But commercial tools generally suffer from two key issues: price and flexibility. Cost can quickly become an issue because the more types of platform and number of hosts that you are managing, the greater the cost. Commercial tools are also usually closed source and are limited to the features available to them, meaning that if you want to extend them, do something custom or specific to your environment, you need to request a new feature, potentially with a waiting period and associated cost.

Free and Open Source Software (FOSS) systems and configuration management tools offer an alternative to both custom and commercial solutions, offering two key opportunities for organizations:

- They are open and extensible.

- They are free!

With FOSS products, the tool's source code is at your fingertips, allowing you to develop your own enhancements or adjustments. You are also part of a community of developers who share the vision for the development of that tool. And you and your organization can in turn contribute to that vision. This ability to shape the direction of the tools you are using can certainly result in a more flexible outcome for your organization.

The price tag is also obviously an important consideration for the purchase of any tool. While you sacrifice paid support for many tools, you do get the tool itself at no cost. Additionally, the active Puppet community can and does provide support. With the price of many commercial configuration management tools running into hundreds of thousands of dollars, the potential cost savings from the use of an open source tool can be substantial.

In the configuration management space, a variety of open source tools are available, in various stages of development and maturity. Some of the key products in this area are

- *Puppet* (http://puppet.reductivelabs.com/):

  A configuration management tool written in Ruby with a client-server model that uses a declarative language to configure clients.

- *cfengine* (http://www.cfengine.org/):

  One of the first open source configuration management tools, released in 1993, it also has a client-server model and is commonly used in educational institutions.

- *LCFG* (http://www.lcfg.org/):

  A client-server configuration management tool that uses XML to define configuration.

- *Bcfg2* (http://trac.mcs.anl.gov/projects/bcfg2):

  A client-server configuration management tool written in Python. It uses specifications and the client responses to configure target hosts.

This book focuses on implementing and using one of these open source products, Puppet, to manage the configuration of your hosts, applications, daemons, and services.

What Is Puppet?

Puppet is an open source Ruby-based systems and configuration management tool relying upon a client-server deployment model. It is licensed using the GPLv2 license and is principally developed by Luke Kanies. Kanies has been involved in Unix and systems administration since 1997, and Puppet has developed from that experience. Unsatisfied with existing configuration management tools, Kanies began working in tool development in 2001 and in 2005 founded Reductive Labs, an open source development house focused on automation tools. Shortly after this, Reductive released their flagship product, Puppet.

What Makes Puppet Different?

Many systems and configuration management products, for example, cfengine, work in a similar manner. So what makes Puppet different? Puppet's defining characteristic is that it speaks the local language of your target hosts. This allows Puppet to define systems administration and configuration tasks with generic instructions on the Puppet server. These instructions are often called *recipes*.

Puppet's recipe syntax allows you to create a single script that allows you to create a user on all your target hosts. In turn, this recipe is interpreted and executed on each target host using the correct local syntax for that host. For instance, if the recipe is executed on a Red Hat Linux server, the user would be created with the useradd command. If the same recipe is executed on a FreeBSD target, the adduser command would be executed. Because Puppet recipes are so portable, community members and contributors share recipes for a variety of activities on the Puppet website, mailing list, and IRC channel!

The next area Puppet excels in is flexibility. As a result of its open source nature, you always have free access to Puppet's source code, meaning if you have a problem and you have the skills to do so, you can alter or enhance Puppet's code to suit your environment. Additionally, community developers and contributors regularly enhance and add to the functionality of Puppet. A large community of developers and users also contribute to providing documentation and support for Puppet.

Puppet is also readily extensible. Functions to support custom packages and configuration unique to your environment can be quickly and easily added to your Puppet installation. In addition, the Puppet community regularly adds code and packages that you can modify or incorporate into your environment.

I'll show you just how easy this is in Chapter 7. These additions can also be readily made without changing the core Puppet code, allowing you a clear upgrade and support path as Puppet develops.

Finally, Puppet makes use of another Ruby-based tool, Facter (http://reductivelabs.com/projects/facter/). Facter is a system analysis tool that allows you to query and return information about hosts that you can use in your Puppet configuration as variables. This means you can write generic configuration instructions and use Facter-returned variables to ensure the right values are configured on the right host. This precludes the need for external databases, configuration files, or directories. I'm going to look at Facter in more detail in Chapter 3 and how to add your own "facts" in Chapter 7.

How Does Puppet work?

With Puppet, central servers, called *Puppet masters*, are installed and configured. Client software is then installed on the target hosts, called *puppets* or *nodes*, that you wish to manage. Configuration is defined on the Puppet master, compiled, and then pushed out to the Puppet clients when they connect.

To provide the client-server connectivity, Puppet uses XML-RPC web services running over HTTPS on TCP port 8140. To provide security, the sessions are encrypted and authenticated with internally generated self-signed certificates. Each Puppet client generates a self-signed certificate that is then validated and authorized on the Puppet master.

Note ➡ Puppet currently uses XML-RPC web services, but at the time of writing a significant update and refactor of the code was taking place to migrate it to a REST-based web services model (http://en.wikipedia.org/wiki/Representational_State_Transfer). This migration should provide much more efficient and elegant web service functionality.

Thereafter each client contacts the server, by default every half hour, to confirm that its configuration is up to date. If new configuration is available or the configuration has changed, it is recompiled and then applied to the client. If required, a configuration update can also be triggered from the server, forcing configuration down to the client. If any existing configuration has varied on the client, it is corrected with the original configuration from the server. The results of any activity are logged and transmitted to the server.

You can see Puppet's client server model in Figure 1-1.

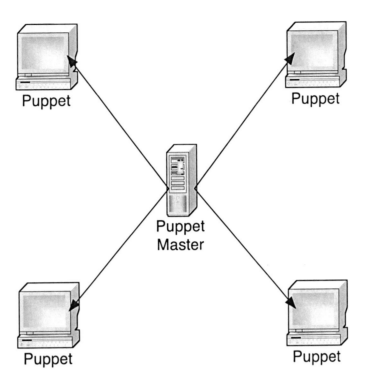

Figure 1-1. Puppet client-server model

Puppet, however, is more than just a client-server configuration management tool—it's a tripartite architecture combining a declarative language, transactional layer, and resource abstraction layer. Let's take a closer look at each.

A Declarative Language

At the heart of how Puppet works is a language that allows you to articulate and express your configuration. Your configuration components are organized into entities called *resources*, which in turn can be grouped together in *collections*. Resources are made up of a *type*, *title*, and a series of *attributes*. You can see an example of a simple resource in Listing 1-1.

Listing 1-1. A Puppet Resource

```
file { "/etc/passwd":
        owner => "root"
}
```

The resource in Listing 1-1 alters the configuration of the /etc/passwd file, changing its ownership to the root user. Inside Listing 1-1 the type being used is the file type. The resource type tells Puppet what type of resource you are managing, for example, the user and file types that are used for managing user and file operations on your nodes, respectively. Puppet comes with a number of resource types by default including types to manage files, services, packages, cron jobs, and file systems, among others. Inside our type we've specified the file to be managed, /etc/passwd; this becomes the title of our resource. When referring to the resource in other parts of our configuration, we'd reference this title. Lastly, we've specified a single attribute, owner, which tells Puppet to set the ownership of the file to the root user.

Note ➡ As you'll learn in Chapter 7, you can also extend Puppet to add your own resource types.

We can extend beyond these single resources with collections. Collections allow you to group together many resources; for example, an application such as Apache is made up of a package, a service, and a number of configuration files. Puppet calls these collections *classes*. Each of these components would be represented as a resource (or resources) and then collected together in a class and applied to a node.

The Puppet language also defines the nodes you wish to configure. After a client is connected to Puppet, a node definition can be created that defines what resources and collections of resources are applied to each node. This allows you to apply appropriate configuration to all nodes running a particular platform or a particular service, for example, specifying all resources required for Red Hat Enterprise Linux nodes or all configuration required for a database or web server.

The Puppet language also allows the use of features you'll find in many programming languages, such as variables, arrays, and conditional statements and clauses. We'll examine Puppet's language in detail in Chapter 3.

A Transactional Layer

Puppet's transactional layer provides the engine of the Puppet client-server deployment. Configurations are created and can be executed repeatedly on the target hosts. The Puppet application architecture describes this sort of configuration as *idempotent*, meaning multiple applications of the same operation will yield the same results.

Puppet is not fully transactional; your transactions aren't logged (other than informative logging) and hence you can't roll back transactions as you can with many databases. You can, however, model transactions in a noop (no operation) mode that allows you to test the execution of your changes without actually making any changes.

A Resource Abstraction Layer

Lastly, Puppet provides an abstraction layer between your platform and the description of your configuration. The resources defined in Puppet to configure your nodes are independent from the commands, formats, and syntax required to configure those resources locally on your nodes. So it does not matter whether you want to create a user on one of many platforms, Puppet considers the definition of that user to be identical.

Puppet does this abstraction using *providers*. Providers are implementations of resource types. In the provider model, a resource is defined in Puppet. The resource is then set to be applied on a node or nodes. Puppet then detects the platform of the node, and the appropriate provider for that platform is then called and used to actually implement the configuration on the node. For example, when creating a user, we define a user type resource in Puppet. We then tell Puppet that we want to create that user on all Mac OS X and OpenBSD nodes. Then when an OS X node connects, the OS X user provider is called and the user created. When an OpenBSD node connects, the OpenBSD user provider is called and the user created. Some platforms share providers, for example, managing files on many platforms is similar, if not identical. Some other resource types, for example, the package resource type, which installs and manages software packages, have numerous providers, as package management is different on a variety of platforms.

Puppet Performance and Hardware

Understanding of Puppet's scalability and performance is still immature at the time of writing. There are two facets to performance management—the number of nodes connected and the amount of configuration defined on each node. There are no clear-cut guidelines around how many nodes and how much configuration on each can be supported on a single master server or around the scale and capacity of hardware required to run the master. Anecdotal evidence suggests that 50 to 100 nodes with a moderate amount of configuration can be managed on a single CPU master with 2GBs of RAM. More nodes will obviously require scaled up hardware.

Internally Puppet uses the WEBrick web server to interface with clients. The WEBrick server does have performance limitations and hence does not provide a fully scalable solution. As an alternative, Puppet also has the capability of internally making use of the more scalable Mongrel web server instead of WEBrick. A load balancer, such as Apache with mod_proxy or Pound, is then placed in front of Puppet. This allows the use of multiple load-balanced Puppet master instances, which should result in a more scalable solution. Generally, the WEBrick web server no longer performs adequately if you are managing 50 or more nodes, and migration to Mongrel will probably be needed.

Note ➡ In Chapter 6, I'll demonstrate how to replace WEBrick with Mongrel.

Sites have reported that when running Puppet with load balancing and Mongrel, node volumes of 5000 or more are feasible with appropriate hardware.

The Future for Puppet

Lastly, it is very important to remember that Puppet is a young tool and is still in the midst of development and change. The Puppet community is growing quickly, and many new ideas, developments, patches, and recipes appear every day. But this does make it important to keep an eye on the Puppet mailing lists and the IRC channel, #puppet on Freenode, as new enhancements that could help you better manage your configurations appear frequently.

Resources

There are a number of useful resources available to get you started with Puppet.

Web

- *Puppet documentation*:

  http://reductivelabs.com/trac/puppet/wiki/DocumentationStart

- *Puppet FAQ*:

  http://reductivelabs.com/trac/puppet/wiki/FrequentlyAskedQuestions

- *About Puppet*:

  http://reductivelabs.com/trac/puppet/wiki/AboutPuppet

- *Introduction to Puppet*:

  http://reductivelabs.com/trac/puppet/wiki/PuppetIntroduction

- *Who is using Puppet*:

  http://reductivelabs.com/trac/puppet/wiki/WhosUsingPuppet

Mailing Lists

- *Puppet mailing lists*:

  http://reductivelabs.com/trac/puppet/wiki/GettingHelp

IRC

- *Puppet IRC channel*:

  irc://irc.freenode.net/puppet

CHAPTER 2

Installing and Running Puppet

This chapter focuses on installing and running Puppet master servers and clients (also known as nodes). There are a variety of methods you can use to install Puppet masters and clients: from source, packages, or as a Ruby Gem. This chapter will take you through the steps required for installation using each of these methods.

The Puppet server and clients are designed to run on Unix and Linux platforms; currently there is no port for Windows (although it may be possible to run Puppet under Cygwin). This book will only cover installation on Unix and Linux platforms. Both the master server and the clients will run successfully on a variety of BSD flavors, Linux distributions, Sun Solaris, Mac OS X, and indeed most Unix-like platforms that support Ruby.

The chapter will also take you through configuring and running both the Puppet master and client. By the end of this chapter, you should have an introduction to how both the master and clients can be configured. You will also be able to start and stop the master and clients on a variety of platforms.

Note ➡ When referring to the Puppet client, we'll distinguish between the terms *client* and *node*. The term *client* refers to the Puppet client daemon that connects to the Puppet master and retrieves the configuration. The term *node* refers to the underlying host to which configuration is applied.

Installation Prerequisites

The process of installing Puppet's master and client components is quick and easy, but you will need to install some prerequisites first. The prerequisites are required for both hosts that run the Puppet master or client (or both—your Puppet master can also be a Puppet node). These prerequisites include the Ruby interpreter, select Ruby libraries, and Facter.

Installing Ruby

As Puppet is a Ruby-based application, the first thing you need to ensure you have installed is Ruby and a few key Ruby libraries. These days, many Linux and other Unix-like platforms come with a Ruby package, and you can install this package and any required library packages. If your distribution does not have a package, you can install Ruby from source.

Installing Ruby from Source

You can download the latest Ruby source package from http://www.ruby-lang.org/en/downloads/. To support Puppet, you will need at least Ruby version 1.8.1 or higher. The current Ruby release, at the time of writing, is 1.8.6. Download the source package and unpack it.

```
# wget ftp://ftp.ruby-lang.org/pub/ruby/ruby-1.8.6.tar.gz
# tar -zxf ruby-1.8.6.tar.gz
```

Change into the resulting directory and configure the package.

```
# cd ruby-1.8.6
# ./configure
```

By default, on most systems the Ruby binary will be installed into /usr/local/bin. You can override this with the --prefix configure option like so:

```
# ./configure --prefix=/usr
```

Here I've specified /usr as the target prefix directory. Next, we need to make and install the Ruby files like so:

```
# make
# make install
```

You can now test that Ruby is installed by executing the following:

```
# ruby --version
ruby 1.8.6 (2007-03-13 patchlevel 0) [i686-linux]
```

If your Ruby version is returned, installation has been successful. If it is not returned, confirm the ruby binary is in your path or check any error messages from the make and/or installation process. Installing Ruby in this manner will install all of the required libraries that Puppet needs to function properly.

Installing Ruby and Ruby Libraries from Packages

Many Linux distributions and Unix operating systems have Ruby packages available for them. These include Red Hat Enterprise Linux and Fedora, Debian, Ubuntu, SuSE, and Mandriva. Some distributions bundle all the required Ruby binaries and libraries in a single package. Other distributions separate the core development environment and the libraries into individual packages. In Table 2-1, I have detailed the package and/or port names for the required packages for a variety of BSD and Linux distributions.

Table 2-1. Package Names for Ruby and Ruby Libraries

OS	Ruby	Ruby Libraries	Additional Package
Debian	ruby	libruby libopenssl-ruby	libxmlrpc-ruby
FreeBSD	ruby		
Gentoo	ruby		
Mandriva	ruby		
NetBSD	ruby		
OpenBSD	ruby		
Red Hat	ruby	ruby-libs	
SuSE	ruby		
Ubuntu	ruby	libruby libopenssl-ruby	libxmlrpc-ruby

So, if we're installing Ruby and its libraries on a Red Hat Fedora host, we need to use its package management system to install the ruby and ruby-libs packages like so:

```
# yum install ruby ruby-libs
```

Installing the Ruby package and libraries may not always install all of the required libraries. If the following base libraries are not installed as part of your base Ruby installation, you may need to selectively install the missing libraries.

- base64
- cgi
- digest/md5
- etc
- fileutils
- ipaddr
- openssl
- strscan
- syslog
- uri
- webrick
- webrick/https
- xmlrpc

The two libraries that are often not packaged with distributions are the Ruby OpenSSL Library and Ruby XMLRPC Library. You can confirm if both these libraries are installed by running the following commands:

```
# ruby -ropenssl -e "puts :installed"
# ruby -rxmlrpc/client -e "puts :installed"
```

If both commands return `installed`, then both libraries are installed. If they return

```
ruby: no such file to load - packagename (LoadError)
```

where *packagename* is the name of the package, `openssl` for example, whose presence is being tested, you will need to install the missing libraries.

Tip ➡ If you want to test for the presence of any library, simply specify the library name as the value of the -r variable in the `ruby` command.

In Table 2-1, I've also listed, for some distributions, additional packages that are needed to support a Puppet installation. For example, in the case of Debian and Ubuntu, you can install the `libopenssl-ruby` package to add the Ruby OpenSSL Library and the `libxmlrpc-ruby` package to add the Ruby XMLRPC Library.

Caution ➡ Not all packages available are the most up-to-date versions of software. Always check that the version installed is suitable to run any required software and functionality.

Ruby is also available for Sun Solaris and ships with the Solaris 10 Community release (`http://www.sun.com/software/solaris/freeware/`). For Mac OS X, you can use the MacPorts or FinkCommander applications to install Ruby. Or if your Mac runs the Leopard OS X release, Ruby should be bundled as part of the operating system. It is possible to install Ruby on HP UX, and you can find a port at `http://hpux.connect.org.uk/hppd/hpux/Shells/ruby-1.8.4/`. Lastly, you can compile Ruby versions later than 1.8.5 on AIX.

Installing Facter

Puppet relies on the Facter tool to provide information about hosts. Facter is also developed by Puppet's developers, Luke Kanies and Reductive Labs, and is written in Ruby. It is a cross-platform Ruby library for returning "facts" about the operating system of a host, for example, IP addresses, operating system versions, and the like. It can be installed from source, or some platforms have a Facter package available. I'll demonstrate both options.

Installing Facter from Source

Facter is available as a source package from the Reductive Labs site at `http://www.reductivelabs.com/downloads/facter/`. Download the latest package, release 1.3.8 at the time of writing, and unpack the archive.

```
# wget http://www.reductivelabs.com/downloads/facter/facter-1.3.8.tgz
# tar -zxf facter-1.3.8.tgz
# cd facter-1.3.8
```

Now install the `facter` binary and libraries using the `install.rb` script.

```
# ruby install.rb
```

You can confirm that Facter is installed and working like so:

```
# facter --version
1.3.8
```

This should return the version of the currently installed Facter.

Running facter without any options will return a list of all the facts and their values that are currently available on your host.

Installing Facter from Package

Not all platforms have a Facter package available, but some do. You can install this package with your chosen platform's package management system. Table 2-2 presents a list of all of the platforms with Facter ports or packages available at the time of writing.

Table 2-2. Facter Packages

PlatformFacter	Package Name
Debian	facter
Fedora	facter
FreeBSD	facter
Gentoo	facter
OpenBSD	ruby-facter
Ubuntu	facter

Tip ➡ If you install Facter on Debian, you may also want the lsb-release package (if it is not already installed). This package provides Facter with Linux Standard Base facts that help you identify specific Debian and derived distributions. Most other Linux distributions install this package by default, for example, Ubuntu and Red Hat (redhat-lsb).

For example, if you are using Gentoo, you can add the Facter package by merging it like so:

```
# emerge facter
```

For RPM-based distributions, there are three sources of RPM files available: at Reductive's site (`https://reductivelabs.com/downloads/rpm/`), at Dag Wieers RPM repository (`http://dag.wieers.com/rpm/packages/facter/`), and via Red Hat employee David Lutterkort's repository (`http://people.redhat.com/dlutter/yum/`).

There is also a Facter package available for OS X. The package combines both Facter and Puppet and can be downloaded from `http://reductivelabs.com/downloads/packages/OSX/`. Reductive reports that the build appears to be stable, but the OS X version has not been extensively tested.

You can confirm Facter is installed by running it with the `--version` option to return the release.

Installing RDoc

You may want to optionally install the RDoc package. RDoc is the Ruby Standard Documentation System. It allows Ruby applications to return help text and documentation when prompted. RDoc may come with Ruby versions later than 1.8.2, and many platforms still have a separate package for RDoc. If you don't have RDoc installed, your Facter or Puppet binaries will not return any help text when prompted, for example:

```
# facter --help
No help available unless you have RDoc::usage installed
```

You can confirm whether you have RDoc installed or not by checking for the presence of the RDoc usage library like so:

```
# ruby -rrdoc/usage -e "puts :installed"
installed
```

If the command returns `installed`, you already have RDoc. But if it returns

```
ruby: no such file to load -- rdoc/usage (LoadError)
```

you will need to install RDoc if you wish documentation to be returned by the Puppet binaries.

In Table 2-3, I have listed those platforms that provide separate RDoc packages.

Table 2-3. RDoc Packages

PlatformRDoc	Package Name
Debian	rdoc
FreeBSD	ruby-doc-stdlib
Gentoo	rdoc
NetBSD	ruby-doc-stdlib
Red Hat	ruby-rdoc
Ubuntu	rdoc

Your package management system may also prompt you to install some dependencies when you install RDoc; for example, the irb package is also commonly required.

Installing Puppet

As I discussed in Chapter 1, the software elements of Puppet consist of a server and a client. Now that you've installed the required prerequisites, I am going to demonstrate how to install Puppet. You can install Puppet via source, from a package on some platforms, and using a Ruby Gem. I'll demonstrate how to use all methods.

Tip ➡ If you build your servers with tools like Jumpstart or Kickstart, you can also include the Puppet client (and its prerequisites) as part of your default build. That'll help you to quickly add nodes to your Puppet environment.

Installing from Source

The latest source package for Puppet is available from the Reductive Labs site at http://reductivelabs.com/trac/puppet/wiki/DownloadingPuppet. It is available in two packages—stable and latest. The stable source package is the current production version, and the latest version represents the latest development release of Puppet. For your production environments, I recommend that you install the stable package and reserve the latest version for your test or development environment.

Tip ➡ Puppet is actively developed, and version upgrades are frequent. I recommend regularly checking back for updates and changes. Puppet's latest source code is also available via Reductive Lab's Git site at `http://reductivelabs.com/git/puppet/`. This is the latest code and may have issues with stability, but it represents the cutting edge of development and features.

The source package contains both the Puppet server and client—so we only need to download one file.

```
# wget --no-check-certificate https://reductivelabs.com/downloads/puppet/ ➡
puppet-0.22.4.tgz
```

Note ➡ You might need to add the `--no-check-certificate` option to wget if your host can't validate Reductive Lab's certificate.

At the time of writing, the latest stable Puppet version is 0.22.4, and the current development release is 0.23.2. Unpack the downloaded file and change into the resulting directory.

```
# tar -zxf puppet-0.22.4.tgz
# cd puppet-0.22.4
```

Puppet is installed by executing the `install.rb` script contained in the package by running it with Ruby like so:

```
# ruby install.rb
```

You can then confirm Puppet is installed by running

```
# puppet --version
0.22.4
```

The Puppet server and client are now both installed, and you can refer to the sections "Configuring puppetmasterd" or "Configuring puppetd" for configuration instructions.

Installing Puppet by Package

Puppet is available as a package for a number of platforms, but not all. At the time of writing, packages are available for Debian, FreeBSD and OpenBSD, Gentoo, Red Hat Fedora, and Ubuntu as part of their port or package management systems. Some packages contain both the server and the client, while others have separate packages for each. I've listed all the package names for each platform in Table 2-4.

Table 2-4. Puppet Packages

PlatformPuppet	Server	Puppet Client
Debian	puppetmaster	puppet
Fedora	puppet-server	puppet
FreeBSD	puppet	NA
Gentoo	puppet	NA
OpenBSD	ruby-puppet	NA
Ubuntu	puppet	NA

Caution ➡ Remember that packages available for platforms may not always be up to date! You should confirm the exact version number of any package you install to ensure it is sufficiently up to date.

There are also packages available for other platforms that are not delivered with the platform itself. You can find packages for SuSE at http://download.opensuse.org/repositories/system:/management/. There are two packages, puppet for the client and puppet-server for the server.

Packages for OS X are available from Reductive Labs at http://reductivelabs.com/downloads/packages/OSX/. These packages contain both Puppet and Facter. As I mentioned earlier, the package appears stable but has not been extensively tested.

Reductive also runs an RPM repository that has RPMs, Source RPMs, and specification files that you can use to install on any RPM-based platforms, for example, Red Hat

Enterprise Linux, CentOS, and Mandriva. You can find the repository at
`https://reductivelabs.com/downloads/rpm/`. The Puppet client is installed with an RPM
called puppet and the server with an RPM called `puppet-server`.

An employee of Red Hat, David Lutterkort, also maintains a yum repository that has
RPMs available for Fedora Core 5, 6, and 7 and Red Hat Enterprise Linux 4 and 5. The
yum repository is at `http://people.redhat.com/dlutter/yum/`.

There are Puppet packages for Solaris available from
`http://reductivelabs.com/downloads/packages/SunOS/` or from the Blastwave project at
`http://www.blastwave.org/packages/puppet`. There are packages available for both x86 and
sparc systems.

Lastly, though not supported, there is some documentation about installing Puppet on
AIX at `https://reductivelabs.com/trac/puppet/wiki/PuppetAIX`.

Caution ➡ Always remember that third-party repositories should be used at your own risk.

Installing Puppet from a Ruby Gem

You can also install Puppet from a Ruby Gem. RubyGems is a package manager for Ruby,
much like the Perl CPAN repository. Before you can use it, you may need to install it. You
can check whether you have it installed by the presence of the gem binary.

RubyGems is available as a package with many platforms' package management
systems; you can see a full list of these platforms in Table 2-5.

Table 2-5. RubyGems Packages

PlatformRubyGems	Package Name
Debian	rubygems
FreeBSD	rubygems
Gentoo	rubygems
NetBSD	rubygems

(Continued)

PlatformRubyGems	Package Name
OpenBSD	rubygems
Red Hat	rubygems
SuSE	rubygems
Ubuntu	rubygems

If there is not a RubyGems package for your platform, you can also download a source package and compile it yourself. You can find the RubyGems source package by clicking the downloads link at http://rubygems.org/.

Download the latest version of RubyGems and unpack it.

```
# wget http://rubyforge.org/frs/download.php/20989/rubygems-0.9.4.tgz
# tar zxf rubygems-0.9.4.tgz
# cd rubygems-0.9.4
```

We use the ruby binary to run the setup.rb script to install RubyGems like so:

```
# ruby setup.rb
```

This will install the gem binary, which we can check is functioning like so:

```
# gem --version
0.9.4
```

Once you have installed RubyGems, you can use the gem binary to install Gems such as Puppet. The Puppet Gem is located on the Reductive Labs site, and you can install it like so:

```
# gem install --remote --source http://reductivelabs.com/downloads puppet
```

Note ➡ When installing Puppet from a Gem, the Facter Gem will also be installed as a dependency.

At the end of the installation process, both the Puppet server and client will be installed.

Note ➡ You can also install the very latest cutting-edge Puppet from its Subversion source repository using the instructions you can find at http://www.reductivelabs.com/trac/puppet/wiki/PuppetSource.

Getting Started with Puppet

Now that we've installed Puppet, let's get the Puppet master daemon up and running and add our first node. One of the strengths of the Puppet infrastructure is that most of the functionality will run with default configuration, without any changes required on your behalf. The only two things we need to get Puppet running are a user and group to run it and a very basic configuration to apply to our first node. In this section, we will create that user and group and then look at starting the Puppet master daemon for the first time using our basic configuration.

First, we need to ensure we have a user and group for the master daemon to run as. If you've installed Puppet from a package, generally a user and group, usually both called puppet, will already have been created for you. You can check for this user by using the `id` command like so:

```
# id puppet
uid=503(puppet) gid=503(puppet) groups=503(puppet)
```

You could also check the `/etc/passwd` and `/etc/group` files directly:

```
# grep 'puppet' /etc/passwd
puppet:x:503:503:puppet user:/home/puppet:/bin/bash
```

If the puppet user and group does not exist, you need to create them. I recommend naming both user and group puppet as this is the default Puppet expects. So on a Red Hat host you would create them like so:

```
# groupadd puppet
# useradd -M -g puppet puppet
```

Starting the Puppet Master

If we've got a user and group to run the Puppet master server, we can start it using the puppetmasterd binary.

```
# puppetmasterd
Manifest /etc/puppet/manifests/site.pp must exist
```

You can see that trying to start puppetmasterd has resulted in an error message stating that the manifest, `/etc/puppet/manifests/site.pp`, must exist. A *manifest* is Puppet's term for a text document that defines a particular configuration or configurations. These manifests are then compiled and applied to a Puppet node to set the desired configuration on the node.

Puppet requires a central manifest file, called the *site manifest*, before the master daemon can be started. By default, this site manifest file is called site.pp and is located in the /etc/puppet/manifests directory (you'll learn how to reconfigure this location later in this chapter). This central manifest will ultimately contain all the configuration information required to configure all your nodes, either directly in the file or by including and importing other files.

But we'll discuss your manifest configuration and how to structure it in Chapter 4. For now, we just want to create a simple site.pp file so we can get Puppet started. First, let's create the directory:

```
# mkdir -p /etc/puppet/manifests
```

Now, in Listing 2-1 you can see an example site.pp file.

Listing 2-1. Your First site.pp *File*

```
file { "/etc/passwd":
    owner => "root",
    group => "bin",
    mode  => 644,
}
```

This site.pp file is very simple: it sets the user and group ownership of the /etc/passwd file as well as its permissions. Indeed, our first site.pp file could do anything, we just need a syntactically correct file so we can start the daemon; we will add to it further and look at its syntax in Chapter 3.

Now in Listing 2-2, with our newly created site manifest, let's try to start the master daemon again.

Listing 2-2. Starting the Master Daemon

```
# puppetmasterd --verbose --no-daemonize
info: Starting server for Puppet version 0.23.0
info: Parsed manifest in 0.01 seconds
info: Listening on port 8140
notice: Starting Puppet server version 0.23.0
```

This time we've started puppetmasterd with the --verbose and --no-daemonize options. The --verbose option turns on verbose logging, and the --no-daemonize option forces the master daemon to run in the foreground. This mode is ideal for troubleshooting your master daemon.

Puppet expects to find each node defined in a manifest, either directly in the site.pp file or in another file and imported into the site manifest. The node definitions tell Puppet about each host to be configured and exactly what configuration applies to them; for example, you might have configuration specific to Debian hosts, or to web servers or hosts in a specific location. When you are using node definitions, only the configuration defined to a particular node will be applied to that node.

Puppet detects if you have any nodes defined. If you don't have any defined, as we have here, Puppet turns off node designation. With node designation turned off, all configuration resources (excluding configuration in classes and definitions, which we'll talk about in Chapter 3) defined will be applied to all nodes that connect to the master. As we don't have any nodes, nor any substantive configuration, it's easiest to turn off nodes until we're ready to define our first node. We'll look at node definition in Chapter 3.

From Listing 2-2, you can see the master daemon has started and is listening on TCP port 8140. You'll need to open this port in any firewall you have running on the local host. If the port is open and the master daemon has started without any error messages, you're now ready to connect your first node.

Starting the Puppet Client

Unlike the Puppet master daemon, the Puppet client daemon runs as the root user, allowing it to perform the required configuration actions on your Puppet node. The first time you start a node, it will generate a local self-signed certificate, connect to a master server (which, in addition to distributing configuration to nodes, also acts as a Certificate Authority) you specify, and request that the certificate be signed.

Tip ➡ Puppet relies on SSL to talk between client and server. You need to ensure that the time on your server and client is correct and appropriately synchronized to ensure SSL functions correctly.

Once the certificate is signed, the node will request whatever configuration is specified for that node. The master server will then compile and deliver that configuration. The configuration is then implemented on the node. The Puppet client will then periodically, by default every 30 minutes, check the master to see whether the configuration defined there is unchanged. If it has changed, the client will request a recompilation of the configuration, and the new configuration will be implemented on the node.

Tip ➡ If you're running the Puppet client on the same host as the server, your certificate will be automatically signed.

Now, let's start the Puppet client, as demonstrated in Listing 2-3.

Listing 2-3. Starting the Puppet Client

```
# puppetd --server puppetmaster.testing.com --verbose --waitforcert 60
notice: Did not receive certificate
```

We've started the Puppet client daemon with three options, --server, --verbose, and --waitforcert. The --server option tells the client the name of the server to connect to. You should specify the server in the form of a fully qualified domain name. The --verbose option enables verbose output for the client and stops it going into the background and daemonizing.

The last option, --waitforcert, tells the client to check every 60 seconds to see whether a signed certificate is returned from the server. This option is generally only used when you are connecting a new node and tells the client daemon to keep checking the server for a signed certificate. You can see in Listing 2-3 a log message indicating that the client is still waiting for the certificate from the server:

```
notice: Did not receive certificate
```

If you check on your master daemon, you can see a corresponding log message:

```
notice: Host node1.testing.com has a waiting certificate request
```

This message indicates that the client's request to have a certificate signed has been received, and now you need to act on it.

Signing Your Client Certificate

So how does our node get a signed certificate, our node authenticated, and the node configuration delivered? Certificate signing is done on the master server by the puppetca tool. The puppetca tool controls the Puppet Certificate Authority and allows certificate requests to be signed or revoked.

Note ➡ You can also configure Puppet to automatically sign all incoming certificate requests (known as *autosign*), either from every node or using coarse-grained authentication to selectively sign node requests based on hostname or domain. Using both forms of autosign poses a serious security risk as they bypass Puppet's security controls. I don't recommend using autosign. But if you do, you can see more details about autosign and Puppet's certificate management at `http://www.reductivelabs.com/trac/puppet/wiki/CertificatesAndSecurity`.

You can list all of the waiting certificate signing requests like so:

```
# puppetca --list
node1.testing.com
```

You can see the `--list` option has listed our node's signing request. Now, if we want to sign it, we can use the `puppetca` command again like so:

```
# puppetca --sign node1.testing.com
Signed node1.testing.com
```

We specify the option `--sign` together with the hostname of the node whose certificate we wish to sign, in this case `node1.testing.com`. On the next line, we can see the command has returned a message indicating that the certificate is now signed. The node is now authenticated to the server.

If we go back to the client daemon, we will see logging messages indicating that the certificate has been returned and the client has been started.

```
notice: Got signed certificate
notice: Starting Puppet client version 0.23.0
```

Then server will now compile and deliver any configuration for that node to the client daemon to be applied. In our example `site.pp` file in Listing 2-1, we're configuring the `/etc/passwd` file and have changed its group ownership, from the default of `root` to `bin`. You should now see the `/etc/passwd` file has the updated group ownership.

```
# ls -la /etc/passwd
-rw-r--r-- 1 root bin 1579 2007-08-01 19:05 /etc/passwd
```

Now you've got a simple Puppet master daemon running and have your first node connected. If you want you can now jump ahead to Chapter 3 to look at how to use Puppet to configure your hosts, or you can continue to read this chapter to learn more about how to run and configure Puppet.

Running the Puppet Daemons

Like most Unix and Linux applications, the Puppet daemons, puppetmasterd and puppetd, can be started and stopped using your platform's standard spawn process. Indeed, if you've installed Puppet from a package, you'll usually find that the package installation process has added the appropriate links and scripts to start the daemons when your host boots.

If you have manually installed Puppet from source, or your package installation has not provided a control script, you can find a variety of scripts you can use in the Puppet source package in the conf directory. Currently, there are scripts and configuration files for FreeBSD (which can be easily adjusted for other BSD platforms), Gentoo, Red Hat, Solaris, and SuSE. You can easily modify the files available to suit most platforms capable of running Puppet.

Tip ➡ The Puppet daemons also do some signal handling. The Puppet master and client daemons both recognize the SIGHUP signal, which forces the daemons to restart themselves. The SIGINT signal will terminate both the master and client daemons. The Puppet client also processes the SIGUSR1 signal, which causes the daemon to initiate a new connection to the server and check for new configuration.

Configuring Puppet

Your Puppet installation comes with a number of binaries that run the various Puppet functions and daemons. We've already touched on the puppetd, puppetmasterd, and puppetca binaries, but we'll go into more detail on them in the sections that follow. This is not a definitive guide to every configuration option but rather focuses on the key options. For a full reference to every command-line and configuration file option, you can find a guide at http://www.reductivelabs.com/trac/puppet/wiki/ConfigurationReference.

Each Puppet binary can be configured via the command line or via a configuration file or files. In Table 2-6, you can see a list of all the Puppet binaries and their purposes.

Table 2-6. Puppet Binaries

Binary	Description
puppet	A local configuration script interpreter and executor
puppetd	The Puppet client daemon that runs on the managed host
puppetmasterd	The Puppet master daemon that manages the nodes
puppetca	The Puppet Certificate Authority server used to authenticate nodes to the master server
puppetrun	A tool that can connect to clients and force them to run their configurations
filebucket	A client to send files to a Puppet file bucket
ralsh	An interactive Puppet shell for converting current state into Puppet configuration code
pi	Tool to output documentation about Puppet types and providers
puppetdoc	Tool that prints Puppet reference documentation (generally only used within other Puppet tools)

Each binary has a different set of command-line options you can use to run and configure it. The easiest way to see the configuration options used for each binary is by executing the binary with the --help option like so:

```
# puppet --help
```

Note ➡ To get the --help text, you need to have the RDoc library installed as discussed earlier in this chapter.

Puppet configuration can also be managed via configuration file. Puppet's configuration file model is in the style of INI files. Each file is divided into namespace sections, and each section name is enclosed in parentheses and named for the Puppet function it configures; for example, the namespace used to configure the Puppet client daemon is called [puppetd]. The use of namespaces means options can be used in multiple namespaces, if the option is relevant to the binary being configured. For example, you can specify the same option twice, with different values, in the [puppetd] and [puppetmasterd] namespaces, and each binary will use only the configuration option contained in its own namespace.

In Table 2-7, I've listed the key namespaces in the configuration file.

Table 2-7. Configuration File Namespaces

Section	Description
main	General configuration options for multiple elements of Puppet
puppetd	Configuration options related to the Puppet client daemon
puppetmasterd	Configuration options related to the Puppet master daemon

You can see an example of a Puppet configuration file in Listing 2-4.

Listing 2-4. Puppet Configuration File

```
[main]
vardir = /var/lib/puppet
logdir = /var/log/puppet

[puppetd]
localconfig = $vardir/localconfig
```

You can see we've defined two namespaces, [main] and [puppetd], in Listing 2-4 and specified some configuration options in each. Configuration options are structured as follows:

```
option = value
```

Boolean options are structured like so:

```
option = true
```

Or:

```
option = false
```

Each Boolean option is either defined as true or false.

When parsing a configuration file, all binaries will set options contained in the [main] namespace and will then set any options specified in the section named for the binary being executed; for example, the puppetd binary will set all options in the [puppetd] namespace.

You can also see in Listing 2-4 that you can reuse previously defined options in other configuration options by prefixing them with $. For example, we defined the `vardir` option in the `main` section and then reused this value as part of the `localconfig` option in the `puppetd` section.

```
$vardir/localconfig
```

You can also use any configuration option from the Puppet configuration file on the command line by prefixing it with `--`. So to specify the `vardir` option on the command line, we would specify `--vardir` as an argument. Boolean configuration options are specified on the command line using an on/off model like so:

```
# puppetd --trace
# puppetd --no-trace
```

In the first line, the `trace` option is set on, and in the second line, it is disabled by prefixing the option with `no-`.

By default, Puppet binaries will look for their configuration in a file located in the `/etc/puppet/` directory. From version 0.23.0 of Puppet, each binary looks for a configuration file called `puppet.conf` in `/etc/puppet`. In previous versions, each Puppet binary looked for separate files, i.e., the Puppet master daemon looks for the `puppetmasterd.conf` file, the client for `puppetd.conf`, and the Puppet Certificate Authority for `puppetca.conf`.

This transition to a single configuration file is aided by the use of the `--genconfig` option. You can execute each of the Puppet binaries with this flag and a commented, default configuration file will be outputted, and the binary will exit. You can pipe this output into a file to create a configuration file like so:

```
# puppetmasterd --genconfig > /etc/puppet/puppet.conf
```

The resulting output makes an excellent starting point for an initial Puppet configuration.

In this chapter, we're going to focus on running and configuring three of the Puppet binaries; their configuration file options, `puppetmasterd`, `puppetd`, and `puppetca`; and the options contained in the general [main] section of the configuration file. We'll touch on the other binaries and configuration options in later chapters.

Tip ➡ You can see a full list of all configuration options and their functions at `http://www.reductivelabs.com/trac/puppet/wiki/ConfigurationReference`.

The [main] Configuration Namespace

Every Puppet binary will check the configuration file and set any configuration options found in the [main] namespace in your Puppet configuration file. These variables set the high-level options that control Puppet's environment, such as the location of the configuration directory. In Table 2-8, I've listed some of the key options you can configure in the [main] namespace.

Table 2-8. The [main] *Configuration File Section*

Option	Description
confdir	Location of the configuration directory. Calculated based on the user running the binary and defaults to /etc/puppet.
vardir	Location of dynamic data directory. Calculated based on the user running the binary and defaults to /var/puppet.
logdir	Log directory, defaults to $vardir/log.
rundir	Location of Puppet PID files, defaults to $vardir/run.
statedir	State directory, defaults to $vardir/state.
statefile	State file, defaults to $statedir/state.yaml.
ssldir	Location for Puppet's SSL certificates, defaults to $confdir/ssl.
trace	Whether to print stack traces on error, defaults to false.
filetimeout	The frequency in seconds that configuration files are checked for changes.
syslogfacility	Specifies the syslog facility to use, defaults to daemon.

The first options in Table 2-8 specify the location of a variety of Puppet resources. The confdir options tells Puppet where to look for configuration files. The value of this option is used as a default for other directory locations; for example, the default directory for SSL certificates, specified using the ssldir option, is $confdir/ssl. The default value for this option is dependent on the user that is executing Puppet. If the user is root or the user specified in the user option (in the [puppetmasterd] namespace), it defaults to /etc/puppet; otherwise, it defaults to ~.

Other directories that can be specified include the vardir for dynamic Puppet data and the logdir option that specifies the location of Puppet log files. Also configurable are the Puppet state directory and state file using the statedir and statefile options, respectively. The Puppet state directory and file hold the current state of running configuration, and the state file stores the state in YAML (a recursive acronym for YAML Ain't Markup Language—http://yaml.org) format.

The trace option turns on stack tracing for some Puppet errors. It is a Boolean option and defaults to false. The filetimeout option specifies how often in seconds Puppet will check for updates in configuration files; it defaults to 15 seconds. The last option in Table 2-8 allows you to set the syslog facility that Puppet will use. It defaults to daemon.

Note ➡ Puppet also has support for multiple environments, for example, production, testing, and development. There is some documentation available describing multiple environments at http://reductivelabs.com/trac/puppet/wiki/UsingMultipleEnvironments.

Configuring puppetmasterd

The Puppet master daemon is initiated by the puppermasterd binary. This is the core of the Puppet client-server model; the server compiles and provides the compiled configuration to the nodes. In this section, we'll look at some of the command-line flags and configuration file options that can be used to configure the Puppet master daemon.

There are a number of command-line flags you can pass to the binary, and you can see a list of the most useful flags in Table 2-9.

Table 2-9. puppetmasterd *Flags*

Flag	Description
--daemonize I -D	Daemonize the process (default).
--no-daemonize	Do not daemonize the process.
--debug I -d	Enable debugging (leaves process in the foreground).
--logdest I -l *file* I console I syslog	Specify logging destination (defaults to syslog).
--mkusers	Create the initial set of users and directories.
--verbose I -v	Enable verbose output (leaves process in the foreground).
--help I -h	Print help text.
--version I -v	Print the version.

Let's examine the flags in Table 2-9 in more detail. The --daemonize option tells the Puppet master daemon to daemonize the process and is the default behavior of the puppetmasterd binary when executed. The --no-daemonize option flag prevents the process being daemonized and leaving it running in the foreground. The --debug option causes the process to output debugging data. This is useful for troubleshooting. The --logdest flag lets you tell the master daemon where to output logging data; you have the choice of specifying a file name, syslog output, or the console. It defaults to syslog output.

The --mkusers flag only needs to be run once when you first install Puppet. It creates the required puppet user and group for Puppet to run as (if they haven't already been created).

Lastly, the --verbose option outputs all logging messages to the command line. The --help and --version options print the help text and version, respectively.

In the Puppet configuration file, there are also some useful options for the [puppetmasterd] namespace that you can use to configure the Puppet master daemon. You can see these options in Table 2-10.

Table 2-10. puppetmasterd Namespace Options

Option	Description
user	The user who should run the Puppet master daemon
group	The group who should run the Puppet master daemon
manifestdir	The directory to store configuration manifests, defaults to $confdir/manifests
manifest	The name of the site manifest file, defaults to $manifestdir/site.pp
bindaddress	The interface to which to bind the daemon
masterport	The port to run the Puppet master daemon on

The user and group options tell puppetmasterd what user and group to run as; this defaults to puppet in both cases. The manifestdir and manifest options specify the directory for storing manifests and the name of the site manifest file, which default to /etc/puppet/manifests and /etc/puppet/manifests/site.pp, respectively. The bindaddress and masterport options allow you to control what interface and port to bind the daemon to; these default to binding to all interfaces and to port 8140.

Configuring puppetd

The command-line operation of the Puppet client daemon is very similar to the operation of the master daemon. It can be configured both from the command line and via a configuration file, and in this section we'll look at the options that are typically specified for the daemon. In Table 2-11, you can see some of the common command-line flags you can use with puppetd.

Table 2-11. puppetd *Flags*

Flag	Description
--daemonize I -D	Daemonize the process (default).
--no-daemonize	Do not daemonize the process.
--server *name*	Name of the Puppet master server to connect to.
--waitforcert I -w *seconds*	Time in seconds between certificate signing requests.
--onetime I -o	Connect and pull down the configuration once and then exit.
--noop	Run in NOOP or dry-run mode.
--disable	Temporarily disable the Puppet client.
--enable	If disabled, reenable the Puppet client.
--test I -t	Enable some common testing options.
--debug I -d	Enable debugging (leaves process in the foreground).
--verbose I -v	Enable verbose output (leaves process in the foreground).
--logdest I -l *file* I console I syslog	Specify logging destination (defaults to syslog).
--help I -h	Print help text.
--version I -v	Print the version.

The --daemonize option is the default action for the puppetd process; if executed without options, it will run in the background as a daemon. The --no-daemonize option flag prevents the process being daemonized and leaving it running in the foreground. The --server option is used to specify the name of the Puppet master to connect to; it should be specified as a fully qualified domain name. The --waitforcert option only applies, as discussed in the "Starting the Puppet Client" section, for Puppet nodes without a certificate. It indicates the time in seconds in between certificate signing requests to a Puppet master. Once the node has a signed certificate, this option does nothing.

The --onetime option connects the client to the master, requests the node configuration, applies it, and then exits. The --noop option allows dry runs of configuration without actually applying the configuration. This allows you to see what new configuration will do without actually making any changes to the node. Using this with the --verbose option will output logging messages with the proposed changes that you can verify for correctness. On the following line, you can see an example of typical noop output:

```
notice: //File[/etc/group]/mode: is 644, should be 640 (noop)
```

You can see that the notice indicates that the /etc/group file's permissions are 644, but the configuration would change that to 640. The (noop) at the end of the message indicates that no change has been made.

The --disable and --enable options allow you to turn on and off the Puppet client. The --disable option sets a lock file that prevents the Puppet client from running. The same lock file is set by the Puppet client when running as a daemon to prevent the client from running twice. The --enable option removes the lock file and allows the client to run again on its normal schedule, by default checking half-hourly.

The --test option applies a number of common testing options including verbose logging, running in the foreground, and exits after running the configuration once (the --onetime option). The --debug and --verbose options enable debug and verbose output from the daemon, and the --logdest option allows you to specify where log data will be outputted: console, file, or syslog. The option defaults to syslog output. The last two options, --help and --version, print the help text and the version information, respectively.

There are also some options that you can specify in the configuration file to configure the puppetd daemon. You can see some of the available options in Table 2-12.

Table 2-12. puppetd Namespace Option

Option	Description
server *puppet*	The Puppet master server to connect to, defaults to puppet
runinterval *seconds*	The interval between Puppet applying configuration in seconds, defaults to 1800 seconds, or a half-hour
puppetdlockfile *file*	The location of the Puppet lock file
puppetport *port*	The port that the client daemon listens on, defaults to 8139

The server option is the configuration file equivalent of the command-line --server option and allows you to specify the Puppet master server to connect to; it defaults to puppet. The runinterval option controls how often configuration is applied to the Puppet node. It is from this option that Puppet gets the default half-hourly application of configuration. The option is in seconds and defaults to 1800 seconds.

The puppetdlockfile option specifies the location of the lock file used by the --disable option to control the running of the Puppet client. The option defaults to $statedir/puppetdlock. The puppetdport option controls what port the client daemon binds to; by default this is 8139.

Configuring puppetca

The puppetca binary's primary purpose is to control and interact with the puppetmasterd's built-in Certificate Authority. Its principal purpose, if you don't use the automatic signing of certificates (which is turned off by default), is to sign incoming requests from Puppet clients to authenticate new nodes.

Caution ➡ As discussed, autosigning of certificates is dangerous, as anyone can authenticate to your Puppet master. If you want to autosign certificates, use per-host authentication to only authenticate those hosts you identify. See http://www.reductivelabs.com/trac/puppet/wiki/CertificatesAndSecurity for more details.

We've already seen puppetca's primary function when we connected our first node to Puppet, listing and signing the certificate requests of new nodes using the --list and --sign options.

```
# puppetca --sign node1.testing.com
```

You can specify more than one node on the command line, and you can also sign all outstanding certificate requests by specifying the all keyword like so:

```
# puppetca --sign all
```

You can also see some other useful command-line flags in Table 2-13.

Table 2-13. puppetca Flags

Flag	Description
--revoke I -r *host*	Revoke a node's certificate.
--clean I -c *host*	Remove a node's certificate from the master.
--generate I -g *host*	Generate a client key/certificate pair.
--debug I -d	Enable debugging (leaves process in the foreground).
--verbose I -v	Enable verbose output (leaves process in the foreground).
--help I -h	Print help text.
--version I -v	Print the version.

The --revoke option revokes a client's certificate. You can specify a decimal number, the certificate's hexadecimal code, or the hostname of the client node. The certificate is added to Puppet's Certificate Revocation List (CRL). You can specify the CRL using the cacrl option in the puppetmasterd namespace. The master daemon needs to be restarted to update the CRL with the revoked certificate.

The --clean option removes all files related to a particular node from the Puppet Certificate Authority. The option is most useful for rebuilding nodes. It removes traces of the old certificate and allows you to submit a new certificate signing request from the client.

The --generate option generates a certificate and key pair for the node or nodes specified on the command line.

You can also control a variety of certificate and SSL-related configuration options such as the key, the naming and location of certificates on both the master and the node, and a variety of other options. You can see these options at http://www.reductivelabs.com/trac/puppet/wiki/ConfigurationReference.

Tip ➡ In the future, you may also be able to have multiple master servers use a single certificate authority. At the moment this isn't fully supported, but you can read about it at http://reductivelabs.com/trac/puppet/wiki/MultipleCertificateAuthorities.

Resources

We've looked at installing and configuration Puppet in this chapter, and there are a number of useful resources and documentation online that can also help with this process.

You can also log tickets and bug reports at Puppet's trac site by registering at `http://reductivelabs.com/trac/puppet/register`.

Web

- *Puppet support*:

  `http://reductivelabs.com/trac/puppet/wiki/GettingHelp`

- *Puppet installation guide*:

  `http://reductivelabs.com/trac/puppet/wiki/InstallationGuide`

- *Puppet configuration reference*:

  `http://reductivelabs.com/trac/puppet/wiki/ConfigurationReference`

Mailing Lists

- *Puppet user mailing list*:

  `http://mail.madstop.com/mailman/listinfo/puppet-users`

CHAPTER 3

Speaking Puppet

In Chapter 2, we installed the Puppet master daemon and a Puppet client, and connected our first node to the master. In the process of connecting that first node, we also created a basic site manifest in the `site.pp` file. Our first manifest was simple and set the user and group ownership and the permissions of the `/etc/passwd` file. But Puppet is capable of much more than simply setting the permissions of a single file. It can install packages, ensure services are configured correctly and started (or stopped), configure applications, and perform numerous other functions.

To carry out such tasks, Puppet uses a powerful declarative language that can describe the required configuration in platform-independent terms. The language is then compiled by the Puppet master and delivered to the client that in turn applies the configuration to the target node.

In this chapter, we're going to delve into Puppet's language and demonstrate how to configure a variety of items and make best use of it to manipulate your nodes. By the end of the chapter, you should have a good understanding of how the Puppet language is syntactically structured. We'll also talk about some language conventions to make your Puppet manifests easier to read and understand.

Throughout this chapter, I also will recommend a number of style guidelines for Puppet syntax. These guidelines have developed in the Puppet community, and the use of them will make it easier for others to understand your configurations. You can see a Puppet style guide at `http://www.reductivelabs.com/trac/puppet/wiki/StyleGuide`.

Caution ➡ This chapter is correct at the time of writing and represents an explanation of the core of the Puppet language. But Puppet is a growing and developing language. Syntax changes, new grammar is introduced, and new functionality developed. I recommend you regularly check the Puppet web site and the documentation for updates.

Defining Configuration Resources

The basic configuration declaration in Puppet is called a *resource*. Let's take another look at the contents of the manifest file we created in Chapter 2. You can see it repeated in Listing 3-1.

Listing 3-1. Our First Resource

```
file { "/etc/passwd":
      owner => "root",
      group => "root",
      mode  => 644,
}
```

Listing 3-1 is a simple example of a Puppet configuration resource. Resources are configuration items you want to manage on your nodes. Resources could include items like files, services, cron jobs, users, and groups. Each resource is made up of a type, a title, and attributes.

Let's break Listing 3-1 down. The first statement, `file`, is the resource type. The resource type indicates the type of configuration resource you want to manage on your node, in this case files. Each type has its own set of attributes; for example, the `mode` attribute is used by the `file` type to set file permissions. There are also some special attributes, called *metaparameters*, which can be applied to all resource types.

After we've specified our resource type, we open a set of curly braces. These braces will hold the resource title and attributes.

Resource Titling

The resource title is the field before the colon in our resource. In Listing 3-1, the title is `"/etc/passwd"`; in this case, it is also the literal path to configuration item being managed. The resource title is used by Puppet to refer to resources in other parts of your configuration.

Tip ➡ I recommend enclosing all resource titles in double quotes to ensure they are correctly parsed.

The type and title of a resource combine to uniquely identify that resource to Puppet. This is very important because Puppet practices configuration normalization and hence only allows you to manage a resource in one place. In Listing 3-1, we've defined a resource that manages /etc/passwd. If we defined another resource that also managed /etc/passwd, the Puppet client would return a parse error like so (the server also returns a similar error):

```
err: Could not retrieve configuration: Duplicate definition: File[/etc/passwd] ➡
 is already defined in file /etc/puppet/manifests/site.pp at line 6; cannot ➡
redefine at /etc/puppet/manifests/site.pp:12
```

This control ensures that your configuration does not overlap or duplicate anywhere.

Note ➡ But this seems to create a problem—how do you define a resource that needs to be different on different platforms? What if a file needs different permissions on different platforms? Well, Puppet has an answer to this, and you'll see how that is achieved later in this chapter when we look at conditional statements.

But this error message also reveals something interesting. In the error message the resource is referred to as File[/etc/passwd]. What does this mean? In Puppet, the combination of the capitalized resource type and the title of the resource is a unique identifier for that resource. Let's look at this in Listing 3-2.

Listing 3-2. Referring to a Resource in Another Resource

```
file { "/etc/group":
        require => File["/etc/passwd"],
}
```

In Listing 3-2, we've defined another file resource, /etc/group. We've also specified a metaparameter, require. The require metaparameter allows you to specify objects that the resource depends on. Here the resource File["/etc/passwd"] must exist in order to configure /etc/group. Puppet knows we're citing another resource because the resource type has been capitalized, and the title of the resource has been specified in square brackets. This unique identifier tells Puppet precisely which resource is being referenced.

At the start of this section I mentioned that the title in Listing 3-1, /etc/passwd, represented the literal name of the configuration item being managed. You don't always have to use the literal name though. To make it easier to refer to resources, we can specify a symbolic name for our resource as you can see on the following lines:

```
file { "group":
      name => "/etc/group",
      owner => "root",
}
```

On the previous lines we've done two new things. First, we've not used the literal name as the title but rather specified a symbolic name, group. Second, we've specified an attribute called name. The name attribute is common to a number of resource types; for example, both the file and service types can use it. It allows us to specify the literal name, path, or other identifying information of a configuration item. We can then title the resource symbolically to make it easier to reference.

It is important to remember that Puppet only knows what you tell it about resources. If you define a symbolic name, you should always refer to resources by that symbolic name. If you use both literal and symbolic names, Puppet may assume you are managing different resources, for example:

```
file { "passwd":
      name => "/etc/passwd",
}

file { "/etc/passwd":
}
```

The title of the first resource is passwd and the second resource /etc/passwd, but they both manage the file /etc/passwd. But from Puppet's point of view, these are two different resources as they have different titles.

Resource Attributes

After the title, the attributes of the resource are specified. The attributes tell Puppet how to configure resources. We've already seen a few attributes, and each resource type has its own set of attributes; for example, the owner, group, and mode attributes we saw in Listing 3-1 all belong to the file resource type.

Earlier I also mentioned some special attributes, called metaparameters, which can be applied to all types of resources. The require attribute we used in Listing 3-2 is such a metaparameter: it allows you to specify a resource that the resource depends on. You can see a full list of metaparameters at http://reductivelabs.com/trac/puppet/wiki/TypeReference#metaparameters.

Tip ➡ We'll discuss other metaparameters through this chapter.

In Listing 3-3, you can see how attributes are structured, each attribute separated from its value by the => symbols.

Listing 3-3. Attribute and Value Structure

```
attribute   => value,
attribute2  => value,
```

Tip ➡ Each attribute and value pair should end with a comma. The last attribute should end in a comma or a semicolon.

Puppet has some native attribute values, for example, setting an attribute to true or false:

```
force => true,
```

Values can also be user-supplied; for example, the owner attribute would be set to the name of the user who owns a file such as "root". User-supplied attribute values should always be in double quotes.

Note ➡ Another reason to always quote resource titles and the values of user-supplied attributes is that Puppet has a number of reserved words that are used as part of the syntax, such as true, false, class, define, inherit, and so on. If you need to use one of these words in a title or attribute value, you must quote them.

Resource Style

When a resource has only one attribute, it can be declared on a single line as you can see here:

```
file { "/etc/group": owner => "root" }
```

You can see that we've also dropped the trailing comma from the attribute. This style of declaration can be a useful shorthand but sometimes makes it hard to read resource definitions. For this reason, many people use the multiline structure for all resources.

Multiple resources can be configured using a single resource type as you can see in Listing 3-4.

Listing 3-4. Multiple Declaration Resource Statements

```
file {
    "/etc/passwd":
        ensure => present;
    "/etc/group":
        owner => "root",
        group => "root";
}
```

In Listing 3-4, we've used the file resource type and specified two files. These are two separate resources, and we would refer to them in other Puppet resources as follows:

```
File["/etc/passwd"]
File["/etc/group"]
```

Lastly, Puppet resources support the use of sh-style comments. Comments prefixed by the # character can be placed on empty lines or at the end of lines.

```
# This is a comment
ensure => running, # this is also a comment
```

Resource Defaults

You can also set default attribute values that will apply to all resources of that type. This means that you don't need to specify a particular attribute each time you use the resource. Let's look at an example of a default, using the exec resource type that allows you to execute external scripts or programs, on the following line:

```
Exec { path => "/usr/bin:/bin:/usr/sbin:/sbin:/usr/local/bin" }
```

In the exec resource type, the path attribute is used to specify the search path Puppet uses to find these external scripts. It is an attribute that is frequently specified and is hence a good candidate to be set as a default. We can see that it is a default because the resource type has been capitalized. A resource title does not need to be specified as we're not defining the resource, only the attribute or attributes for which you wish to set a default.

The default can be overridden in specific resources by specifying the attribute in the resource, for example:

```
exec { "shell.rb --run": path => "/opt/bin:/opt/sbin" }
```

On the previous line, we would override the resource default for the path attribute for this particular resource.

Collections of Resources

Resources can configure the characteristics of single configuration items on nodes, but most services and applications are made up of multiple resources. For example, a web server consists of the software package, users to run the software, and a variety of configuration, logging, and other files.

Additionally, individual resources configured in Puppet are applied to all Puppet clients that connect to the master. You can't select particular resources and apply them to specific nodes. So, how do we group together resources and apply resources to the appropriate nodes?

Puppet does this by using *resource collections*. Resource collections allow you to gather together resources, assign them to a collection, and then have that collection applied to one or more nodes. There are two types of resource collections: *classes* and *definitions*.

Note ➡ Even inside collections, resources must be unique. You still can't manage the same resource more than once.

A class is a collection of resources that represents a single configuration item on your node, for example, the SSH service or the NFS package. Classes are only evaluated once per node because the configuration item being managed should only exist once.

A definition is similar but represents a collection of configuration items that have multiple representations on your node, for example, configuring Xen instances or virtual hosts on an Apache web server. Definitions can be evaluated multiple times on a single node, each time with different input parameters.

Classes and Subclasses

Let's start by looking at a class in Listing 3-5.

Listing 3-5. Our First Class

```
class apache {
        package { httpd: ensure => installed }

        service { "httpd":
                ensure  => running,
                require => Package["httpd"],
        }
}
```

A class is defined by specifying the class statement followed by the name of the class being defined, which in Listing 3-5 is apache. We then enclose the class in curly braces. Inside the class we can specify a number of resources. The class would then be included in a node's configuration and all resources applied to the target node.

Tip ➡ We'll look at how to configure nodes in the "Creating Nodes" section later in this chapter.

Classes Relationships

Like resources, we can also specify relationships between classes and other resources (as of release 0.23.1 of Puppet). We can see in Listing 3-5 that we've used the require metaparameter to make the httpd service resource dependent on the httpd package resource like so:

```
service { "httpd":
        ensure  => running,
        require => Package["httpd"],
}
```

Here the httpd service resource requires that the resource Package["httpd"] exist. We can also refer to classes in the same manner using a similar syntax:

```
service { "squid":
        ensure  => running,
        require => Class["apache"],
}
```

This specifies the relationship between a class and a resource. In this instance, the squid service requires that the apache class exist. You'll notice that like resource relationships, we've capitalized the class statement to indicate we're referring to another class and encapsulated the name of the class in block brackets.

Class Inheritance

Classes also have a simple inherit-and-override model using parent classes and subclasses. A subclass can inherit the values of a parent class and potentially override one or more of the values contained in the parent. This allows you to specify a generic class and override specific values in subclasses that are designed to suit some nodes; for example, you could have a generic Red Hat Linux class and override certain values in subclasses for different Red Hat versions. You can see an example of inheritance in Listing 3-6.

Listing 3-6. Class Inheritance

```
class redhat {
      service {
            "mdmdp":
            enable => true,
            ensure => stopped,
      }
}

class rhel5 inherits redhat {
      Service["mdmdp"] { ensure => running }
}
```

Here, class redhat is the parent class and defines a service that controls the mdmdp service. It uses the service resource type to enable the mdmdp service at boot time and specify the service must be stopped. We then specify a new class, a subclass called rhel5, that inherits the redhat class but overrides the ensure attribute and specifies that the mdmdp service must be running for all nodes with the rhel5 subclass included.

In addition to inheritance, we can also use the include function to include the contents of a class in another class like so:

```
class proxy {
      include proxysquidguard
      ...
}
```

Here the proxy class would include the proxysquidguard class in addition to whatever other configuration you wish to define.

From Puppet version 0.23.1 a new feature is also available that allows you to add values to attributes in subclasses like so:

```
class proxy {
        service { "squid": require => Package["squid"] }
}

class proxysquidguard inherits proxy {
        Service["squid"] { require +> Package["squidguard"] }
}
```

Here we have defined the proxy class containing the squid service, which in turn requires that the squid package be installed. We have then created a subclass called proxysquidguard that references the squid service but adds an additional package, squidguard, to the require attribute. To do this, we use the +> operator. After this addition, the squid service would now functionally look like this:

```
service { "squid":
        require => [ Package["squid"], Package["squidguard"] ]
}
```

We can also unset particular values in subclasses using the undef attribute value.

```
class proxy {
        service { "squid": require => Package["squid"] }
}

class proxysquidguard inherits proxy {
        Service["squid"] { require => undef }
}
```

Here we again have the proxy class with the squid service, which requires the squid package. In the subclass, we have removed the require attribute using the undef attribute value.

Definitions

The second type of Puppet resource collection is a definition. Definitions should be used for configuration items that have multiple instances on a node, for example, virtual machines or multiple instances of a web service. Definitions are created using the define keyword and support arguments but not inheritance. The best way to think about a definition is as a reusable snippet of configuration that you can call with arguments. As they are designed to be reused, they cannot contain any resources that will have only one instance on a node, like a package or a service.

This reuse is also the key difference between classes and definitions. Classes contain single instances of resources; for example, a class could contain a package resource that defined the httpd package. This package will only exist once on a node and hence would be installed, removed, or managed using a class. But some configuration exists multiple times on your nodes, for example, the httpd server may have multiple virtual hosts defined. You would then create a definition to configure virtual hosts and pass in appropriate arguments to configure each. As long as each set of arguments was different, Puppet would configure the new virtual host every time the definition was evaluated.

Tip ➡ Don't underestimate the power of definitions! They are highly flexible, powerful, and effective and often represent the best method for defining configuration on your nodes. I recommend examining the Puppet recipes at http://reductivelabs.com/trac/puppet/wiki/PuppetRecipes and http://reductivelabs.com/trac/puppet/wiki/CompleteConfiguration to see how definitions are and can be used.

A definition is created by using the define keyword, specifying a title for the definition, and then listing any arguments in brackets. The definition itself is specified next and is enclosed in curly braces. In Listing 3-7, I've demonstrated a definition that runs a script to configure a new virtual host.

Listing 3-7. Definition

```
define newip ( $ip ) {
        exec { "/sbin/ifconfig $title $ip":
        }
}

newip { eth0:
        ip => "11.11.11.11",
}
```

In Listing 3-7, we've created a definition called newip that has an argument of a variable called $ip. Inside the definition we've used the exec resource type that executes an external binary, in this case the ifconfig command. We've specified the variable $ip and used another variable, $title, that contains the resource title.

Note ➡ The $title variable is available in all definitions and contains the title of the resource.

On the next lines we have actually called the newip definition. It is called much like we define a resource type. We've specified the name of the definition being called, the title, in this case eth0 (which is also the value of the $title variable). We then specify the remaining variable in the same format as we would specify attributes in a resource.

If we then use this definition, we'll see a log message on the client much like this one:

```
notice://newip[eth0]/Exec[/sbin/ifconfig eth0 11.11.11.11]/returns: executed ➡
successfully
```

We can see that the definition has executed the exec resource and the appropriate arguments have been passed into the definition to reconfigure our interface with the new IP address.

We can also specify defaults for each of the arguments passed to our definition like so:

```
define config_file(owner = root, group = root, mode = 0644, ➡
source, backup = false, recurse = false, ensure = file) {

    file{ $name:
        mode    => $mode,
        owner   => $owner,
        group   => $group,
        backup  => $backup,
        recurse => $recurse,
        ensure  => $ensure,
        source  => "puppet:///$source"
    }
}

config_file { "/etc/vnc.conf":
        source => "vnc/vnc.conf",
        mode   => "0640"
}
```

Here we've created the config_file definition. We specify a series of default values for some of the arguments we intend to pass to the definition. We then specify a file resource that will accept the arguments. We then invoke the definition for a sample file, /etc/vnc.conf. We specify the source attribute and then we override one of the default arguments we specified, mode, for the definition.

Qualifying Definitions

Qualified definitions allow you to perform a number of useful functions. First, you can refer to definitions that are defined in classes:

```
class virtuals {
      define newip ( $ip ) {
            exec { "/sbin/ifconfig $title $ip":
            }
      }
}

virtuals::newip { eth0:
      ip => "11.11.11.11",
}
```

We've defined a class called virtuals and placed the definition we created in Listing 3-7 into it. We've then used the newip definition and referenced it by qualifying its location. The qualification is done by specifying the name of the class the definition is in and the name of the definition, and separating each with two colons, ::. The definition is then used normally.

We can also use this syntax to set defaults for a definition.

```
virtuals::newip { noop => true }
```

This would set the noop metaparameter for all resources contained in the virtuals::newip definition. The noop metaparameter tells Puppet whether an operation should occur or not in the same manner as the --noop command-line option.

Lastly, we can use definition qualification to specify dependencies.

```
file { "/etc/hosts.conf":
      notify => network::checkhosts[$hostname]
}
```

On the previous line, we've defined a file resource with the notify metaparameter. The notify metaparameter is a trigger; if the file /etc/hosts.conf changes, the network::checkhosts definition will be called, and the $hostname variable passed to it.

Variables

In some of the previous examples you encountered a new concept: variables. Variables are prefixed with a $ and allow you to specify data that can then be used in resources, for example, as the content of a file. There are also some default variables, like $title, that contain the title of the resource.

```
$variable = "string"
```

You should place your variable strings in double quotes, as single-quoted strings will not do any variable interpolation. You can reference other variables in your strings, and Puppet supports the use of brackets, {}, to help highlight variables in strings.

```
$variable = "string ${anothervariable} string ${thirdvariable}"
```

Variables are also used to pass in facts from the Facter application; for example, the variable $operatingsystem is equivalent to the value of the operatingsystem fact returned by Facter. We'll discuss some of these in the "Facts" section later in this chapter.

Variable Scoping

There is some important information you need to know about variables. First, because Puppet is a declarative rather than an imperative language, variables are scoped differently than in some other languages. The principal result of this is that you cannot redefine a variable inside the same scope it was defined in. So you couldn't redefine the $packagelist in the apache class as shown in Listing 3-8.

Listing 3-8. Redefining Variables

```
class apache {
     $packagelist = ["httpd", "openssl", "mod_ssl"]
     package { $packagelist: ensure => installed }

     $packagelist = "httpd"
     service { "httpd":
          ensure  => running,
          require => Package[$packagelist],
     }
}
```

You can see in Listing 3-8 that we've tried to define the $packagelist variable twice. If we were to try to compile and apply this configuration, the Puppet client would return the following error:

```
err: Cannot reassign variable packagelist at /etc/puppet/manifests/classes.pp:6
```

The error also tells us the file and line number in the file where we've tried to redefine the variable.

So what's a scope? Each class, definition, or node introduces a new scope, and there is also a top scope for everything defined outside of those structures. Each structure represents a nonoverlapping scope; for example, class A is one scope, class B is another scope, and node C is yet another scope. You can see this in Listing 3-9.

Listing 3-9. Nonoverlapping Variable Scopes

```
class apache {
    $apachever = 1
}

class apache2 {
    $apachever = 2
}
```

The same variable can be used and defined in both the apache and apache2 classes without generating an error. The same scoping is true of different nodes and definitions.

Variables and Class Inheritance

Variable scope is also important when inheriting classes. If we have a variable of the same name in a class and a subclass, its behavior may not be what you expect. In Listing 3-10, we define two classes with the same variable in them, and then have the second class inherit the first.

Listing 3-10. Variables and Class Inheritance

```
class master {
    $server = "primary"

    file { "/etc/server.conf":
        content => "$server",
          ensure => present,
    }
}

class slave inherits master {
    $server = "secondary"
}
```

In the first class, master, we define the value of the $server as "primary". The second class, slave, inherits the first class, and we try to redefine the value of the $server variable to "secondary". This redefinition will not work because the $server variable remains in the scope that it was created in when the master class is inherited, and hence remains "primary".

There is a workaround for this that makes use of the include function we introduced earlier in this chapter.

```
$server = "primary"

class master {
        file { "/etc/server.conf":
                content => "$server",
                ensure => present,
        }
}

class slave {
        $server = "secondary"
        include master
}
```

First, we define the $server variable in the top scope, outside the scope of both classes. This is because the include function includes the entire stanza of the master class in the slave class. If the variable was defined inside the master class, we'd get an error when the slave class was evaluated because you can't have two definitions of the same variable in a single class.

Next, we define the master class and then the slave class. The slave class, which is a new scope, changes the value of the $server variable and then uses the include function to incorporate the content of the master class. Now when the slave class is evaluated, the value of the $server variable will be "secondary".

Qualified Variables

We can also reference variables assigned in one class in another class. This allows us to use a previously defined variable again by qualifying it as you can see on the following lines:

```
class master {
        $server = "primary"
}

class slave {
        $ms = $master::server
}
```

You can see in the first class, master, we've defined the value of the variable $server as "primary". In the second class, we've created a variable called $ms. The value of this variable is $master::server. This combines the names of the class and variable being referenced, separated by two colons, ::. The resulting value of the $ms variable in the slave class would be "primary".

We can also refer to the top scope of our manifests (i.e., outside of any nodes, classes, or definitions) by using the following syntax:

```
$ms = $::server
```

This syntax will result in the $ms variable being assigned the value of a variable called $server that is set in the top scope.

Caution ➡ Qualified variables are dependent on the order in which Puppet evaluates your configuration. All resources of the same type are evaluated in order of being parsed, in a top-down manner in your manifest files. For example, each class is evaluated in order from top to bottom. This means you can only qualify a variable that has been defined earlier in the manifest. If you try to evaluate a variable defined later in the manifest, a null value will be set.

Variables and Metaparameters

Using variable syntax, you can also set metaparameter defaults for all resources in a class, for example:

```
class start_vhost {
        $noop = true
        exec { "/usr/sbin/start_ws": }
        exec { "/usr/sbin/start_vhost": }
}
```

In the start_vhost class, we've specified the noop metaparameter as a variable and set it to true. In all the resources in the class, in this case the two exec resources, the noop metaparameter will be added and set to true.

Arrays

In addition to variables, Puppet also allows you to define arrays. In Listing 3-5, we defined an array for the $packagelist variable that contained three packages name: httpd, openssl, and mod_ssl; you can see a subset of that class here:

```
$packagelist = ["httpd", "openssl", "mod_ssl"]
package { $packagelist: ensure => installed }
```

Caution ➡ Don't quote titles, in this case $packagelist, that contain arrays. The array will become conflated.

When specified in the resource title of the package resource type (which manages package installation and removal on nodes), the array is expanded. The package resource attribute, ensure, then checks whether all three packages in the array are installed. Anyone familiar with Ruby will recognize Puppet's array syntax: each element in the array is quoted, separated by commas, and enclosed in square brackets.

Arrays can be used in two principal ways: as the value of a variable as we've done in Listing 3-5 or as the value for a number of resource attributes. For example, the user resource type allows multiple groups to be assigned to a user using an array:

```
user { "mail":
        gid    => "mail",
        groups => ["smtpd", "clamav", "spamassasin"],
        ensure => present,
}
```

Here you can see that the value of the groups attribute is an array containing three group names.

We could also use an array to call a definition multiple times.

```
define ruby::libs() {
        package { "ruby-${name}": ensure => installed }
}

ruby::libs { ["ldap", "mysql", "postgres", "sqlite3", "shadow"]: }
```

Here we've created a definition called ruby::libs that has no arguments but will install any package prefixed with ruby- and the value of the $name variable. We then call the definition and use an array as the value of the resource title. The array would be expanded and each array element assigned to the variable $name. The definition would then install each Ruby library package (e.g., ruby-ldap, ruby-mysql, ruby-postgres, etc.).

Conditionals

Puppet also supports conditionals in resources, classes, definitions, and nodes. They are expressed in the form of a selector with a default option. In Listing 3-11, we can see a conditional selector inside a resource.

Listing 3-11. Conditional Selectors

```
service { "apache":
        name => $operatingsystem ? {
                debian  => "apache2",
                redhat  => "httpd",
                default => "apache",
        },
        ensure => running,
}
```

The conditional selector is inside the apache service resource. It is constructed using the ? symbol and followed by a list of selectors and values, each separated by the => symbols much like attributes. Finally, the conditional is enclosed in curly braces.

You can see we've also specified a value called default. This default value will be used if none of the other conditions are met.

In Listing 3-11, we've also used the name attribute. In addition to allowing you to create a symbolic name, as we discussed earlier in this chapter, the name attribute in combination with a conditional also allows you to take into consideration that different target nodes might name a resource differently. Here we are using the value of the $operatingsystem fact to select what name to use for the service. For example, if the $operatingsystem fact on a node returned a value of redhat, the service name would be set to httpd. When configuring this resource on that node, this is the name Puppet would use for the service.

In Listing 3-12, we have set the value of a variable using a conditional selector.

Listing 3-12. Conditional Selector

```
$environment = $domain ? {
        "testing.com"      => "test",
        "uat.com"          => "uat",
        "development.com" => "development",
        default            => "production",
}
```

We've specified that the value of the $environment variable will depend on what is returned using the domain fact, which returns the domain name of the node. In Listing 3-12, if Facter returns testing.com as the value of the domain fact, it should set the $environment variable to test and so on. The last value, default, is the default value to specify for the $environment variable in the event the fact does not return one of the other values.

Tip ➡ Conditionals can be nested. You can put conditional structures inside other conditional structures.

If you don't set a default value and no other value is matched, a parse error is returned by Puppet.

Note ➡ Puppet selectors are case insensitive when matching. You'll also notice that we've quoted the values being tested and the result. This is good practice to ensure the values are interpreted and returned correctly.

There are also two other conditional statements we can use in our manifests: case and if. The case statement allows you to conditionally select larger stanzas of configuration such as resources or classes depending on a value. You can see a case statement in Listing 3-13.

Listing 3-13. Case Statements

```
case $operatingsystem {
        redhat:  { service { "httpd": ensure => running }}
        debian:  { service { "apache": ensure => running }}
        default: { service { "apache2": ensure => running }}
}
```

The case statement in Listing 3-13 uses the operatingsystem fact we introduced earlier in this chapter to return the operating system of the node the configuration is being evaluated on. Each potential value is specified in curly braces and terminated with a colon, for example, redhat:.

Tip ➡ You should enclose some values in double quotes to ensure they are parsed correctly.

For each value, we can then specify a resource that should be defined if that particular operating system is returned. Lastly, we've specified a default value that tells the case statement what resource to apply if the fact doesn't return any of the previously specified values. As with selectors, if you do not specify a default and no values are matched by the statement, Puppet will return a parse error.

The case statement can also test for the presence of a variable, for example:

```
case $definedvariable {
        "true" => { include class }
        default => {}
```

Here if the $definedvariable is present, or true, a class is included. Otherwise, the default action is to do nothing.

Note ➡ Like selectors, case statements perform case-insensitive matching.

The last conditional statement, if, is a very simple if/else statement. The statement only supports Boolean operations (true or false) and Puppet is not currently capable of using comparison operators (such as greater than, less than, not equal, etc.). You can see an if statement in Listing 3-14.

Listing 3-14. If Statements

```
if $server {
  file { "/etc/server.conf": ensure => present }
} else {
  file { "/etc/client.conf": ensure => present }
}
```

Listing 3-14 is a simple Boolean evaluation: If the variable $server is defined, evaluate the first file resource and ensure that the /etc/server.conf file is present. If it is not defined, evaluate the second file resource, which ensures that the /etc/client.conf file is present.

Creating Nodes

We've looked at defining resources and collections of resources in the form of classes and definitions. So how do we assign these resources and collections to particular clients? Puppet does this by defining each client on the master as a node. Resources and resource collections are then assigned to these nodes.

As mentioned in Chapter 2, when no nodes are defined, all resources not in a specific class or definition are applied to the node; for example, if we had a file type resource defined in our site.pp manifest, that would be applied to the node, but a class would not. With nodes defined, you can define nodes on the master and assign classes and definitions to those nodes.

Note ➡ Ultimately, as Puppet develops, node definitions inside your manifests will disappear, and all nodes will be contained externally in a database or a directory like LDAP. We discuss the initial capability to do this in Chapter 6 when we look at external nodes. This move reflects the growing push for centralized asset and configuration management stores in many organizations.

When the Puppet client connects to the master, its hostname is used to try to match it to a node definition. The hostname used is the client certificate we created, which in turn is based on the fqdn fact returned by Facter. Let's see what Facter returns:

```
# facter | grep 'fqdn'
fqdn => node1.testing.com
```

Here we've executed the facter binary, which usually returns a full list of the facts available about that node. We've grep'ed for the fact called fqdn (fully qualified domain name) and discovered it is node1.testing.com. When Puppet created our certificate, it used this value as the hostname used to identify the client to the master.

When connecting, the Puppet client presents this value to the master. The master checks to see whether it matches a node definition. If the fully qualified domain name of the node doesn't match a node definition, it then tries the short name of the host. If the short name of the host doesn't match any node definitions, it looks for a node called `default`. The `default` node is a special definition you can create to hold configuration that should apply to all nodes. Lastly, if no node definition matches and the `default` node isn't defined, the master will return an error indicating that no matching node has been found:

```
err: Could not retrieve configuration: Could not find node1.testing.com with ➥
names node1.testing.com, node1
```

In the error message, you can see the master has indicated that no node called `node1.testing.com` or `node1` is defined on the master.

So how is a node defined? You can see three nodes defined in Listing 3-15.

Listing 3-15. Sample Nodes

```
node 'webserver.testing.com' {
        include apache
}

node 'webserver2.testing.com' inherits 'webserver.testing.com' {
        include mysql, rails

        virtuals::new_vhost { vhost1:
                ip => "11.11.11.11",
                domainname => "vhost2.testing.com"
        }

}

node default {
    include $operatingsystem
    package { "perl": ensure => present }
}
```

In Listing 3-15, we've added some nodes. Each node is identified by the `node` keyword followed by the name of the node and the configuration defined for that node, enclosed in curly braces.

Tip ➥ As discussed, nodes can be identified by their short name or by their fully qualified domain name. If you specify the fully qualified domain name, you should enclose your node name in single quotes to ensure it is parsed correctly.

Inside your node definition, you can add resources, classes, and definitions. Classes are added using the `include` function. In `webserver.testing.com` in Listing 3-15, we've included the apache class. When `webserver.testing.com` connects, the apache class will be applied to the node to configure it. You can include multiple classes with a single `include` function by separating them with commas.

In `webserver2.testing.com`, we've also added a definition, `new_vhost`, which is qualified as being contained in the `virtuals` class. Rather than being added using the `include` function, definitions are specified by name, together with any required parameters.

Node Inheritance

Nodes, like classes, can also inherit the contents of other nodes. In the second node, `webserver2.testing.com`, in Listing 3-15, we've defined inheritance. In the example, `webserver2.testing.com` would inherit the properties of `webserver.testing.com`, meaning that the node would apply the `mysql` and `rails` classes as well as the apache class from `node1`. Inheritance is cumulative; we could define a third node that inherits `webserver2.testing.com`, and the apache, `mysql`, and `rails` classes would all be applied to it.

Nodes can only inherit one other node, rather than multiple nodes, using the `inherit` statement. But you can build a node inheritance model that allows you to group your nodes and apply appropriate configuration to them. This model allows you to assign configuration to nodes via inheritance rather than having to assign it individually to every node.

Note ➡ Using the `include` function, you can also include the contents of other nodes in the current node. This does allow you to inherit the contents of multiple nodes.

For example, node inheritance is often used to define a base node that contains your default configuration for all nodes and have that node inherited by all others. But a more complex model can also be created: a base node, inherited by a series of other nodes that are in turn inherited by a succeeding layer of nodes, each layer becoming more granular than the last. You can see this sort of inheritance model in Listing 3-16.

Listing 3-16. Layered Node Inheritance

```
node basenode {
        include sudo, basepackages
}

node webserver inherits basenode {
        include webservices
}

node databaseserver,databaseserver2, databaseserver3 inherits basenode {
        include dbservices
}

node webmelb inherits webserver {
        include melbourne
}

node dbsyd inherits databaseserver {
        include sydney
}
```

Listing 3-16 shows the definition of a basenode, which includes two classes. We then create four more nodes, webserver, databaseserver, databaseserver2, and databaseserver3, which inherit the classes included in the basenode and add classes of their own. Finally, we define two nodes, webmelb and dbsyd, which inherit the webserver and databaseserver node definitions, respectively. They also include classes of their own. To make this a bit clearer, I've shown the model from Listing 3-16 (with a few more nodes added) in Figure 3-1.

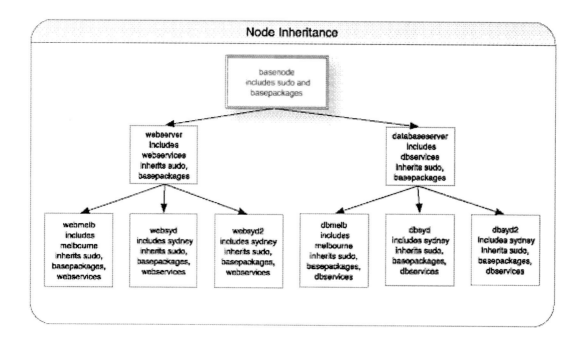

Figure 3-1. Node inheritance

You can see how this sort of structure can allow you to quickly design a deployment model for your nodes that selectively applies the right configuration to the right nodes and is flexible enough to allow you to change the model without having to change the definitions of all your nodes.

Node Inheritance and Variable Scope

Like class inheritance, however, there are issues with node inheritance and variable scoping. Node inheritance is generally only practical for inheriting static classes, for example, those without variables, as you can see in Listing 3-17.

Listing 3-17. Node Inheritance and Variable Scope

```
class master {
        file { "$server":
                ensure  => present,
        }
}

node webserver {
        $server = "primary.conf"
        include master
}

node webserver2 inherits node1 {
        $server = "secondary.conf"
}
```

In Listing 3-17, we've defined a class called master with a file resource entitled
$server. We've then included this class in the definition of webserver and then created
webserver2, which inherits webserver.

In webserver2, we've tried to change the value of the $server variable to "secondary".
But, like class inheritance, the value of the $server variable remains defined in the scope of
webserver and remains with a value of "primary".

As there is for classes, there is a workaround for this issue. The workaround is
somewhat clumsy, as you can see in Listing 3-18.

Listing 3-18. Node and Variable Scoping Workaround

```
class master {
        file { "$server":
                ensure => present,
        }
}

class basenode {
        include master
}

node webserver {
        $server = "primary"
        include basenode
}
```

```
node webserver2 {
      $server = "secondary"
      include base_node
}
```

In Listing 3-18, we've defined a class called master, exactly as we did in Listing 3-15. We've then created another class, called basenode, which includes the master class. We then define two nodes: webserver and webserver2. Each of these nodes includes the basenode class and a different definition of the $server variable. As each node is a separate scope, the variable is applied appropriately in each.

Default Nodes

The last node in Listing 3-15 is the default node. If no node definition is matched, the classes, resources, and definitions in this node are applied to the connecting node. In this case, we're including a class that matches the value of the $operatingsystem fact. For example, if a node connects, the $operatingsystem fact will be evaluated and the result used to include a class. If the fact returned a value of redhat, that class would be included. Lastly, we've included a resource, which ensures that the perl package is installed.

Node Conditionals

Inside nodes we can also use conditionals, as you can see in Listing 3-19.

Listing 3-19. Node Conditionals

```
node 'fileserver.testing.com' {
      case $processorcount {
             1:    { include single }
             2:    { include smb  }
             default: { include single }
      }
}
```

Listing 3-19 shows a node definition for fileserver.testing.com. Inside the definition, we've specified a case statement. The query uses the value of the processorcount fact to determine which of a series of classes to include. If the processorcount fact returns 1, the node will include the single class, if 2, the smb class will be included. We've also specified a default value, which includes the single class, if neither 1 nor 2 is returned by the fact.

Note ➡ Node, class, and definition names must be unique. For example, if you specify a node and a class with the same name, Puppet will return an error indicating that the class can't be evaluated because the node of the same name has already been evaluated.

Virtual Resources

There is another type of resource that we need to look at: virtual resources. Virtual resources are resources that are defined but are not implemented on a client until you specifically configure them to be.

So why is this useful? Well, as we've discovered in this chapter, resources are normalized and can only be configured once. You can't create the same resource in two classes; for example, you can't configure the user james in both the webserver and dbserver classes. Most of the time this isn't an issue—a resource is generally specific to a particular class. But sometimes you have a resource that is needed in multiple unrelated classes. For example, the user james could be both a web site author and a database administrator and therefore needs to be defined in both classes. If we only define the user in one class, it would only be implemented on nodes that included that class. The only way to get around this would be to include both classes on a node, a far from practical solution.

Using *virtual resources* gets around this problem. A virtual resource is only configured once but can be instantiated multiple times in our configuration.

We can identify virtual resources by the @ symbol prefixed to the resource type like so:

```
@user { james: ensure => present }
```

Puppet implements a virtual resource using a feature known as *realization*. Realization offers two methods for marking a virtual resource so that it is implemented. The first is called a collection, and the second uses a function called realize.

Realizing with a Collection

The collection method uses simple selection syntax to select the resources to be realized like so:

```
User <| title == james |>
```

The type of the resource being realized is specified and capitalized. The selection syntax itself is encapsulated in angle brackets and vertical bars. We then specify the selection syntax; here we're realizing a user resource with a title equal to james. We can also specify nonequality like so:

```
User <| title != james |>
```

The previous line would realize all users EXCEPT those with a title equal to james. Selection syntax can also make use of parentheses as well as and/or statements like so:

```
Group <| (title == admin or title == mainframe) |>
```

The last line would realize all group resources with a title of admin or a title of mainframe.
    You can also realize all resources of a type like so:

```
User <|  |>
```

The last line would realize all User type virtual resources.

Realizing with the realize Function

In addition to the collection method, Puppet also has a simple function, realize, for realizing virtual resources. The realize function uses the resource reference, for example, User[james], to refer to a virtual resource that is to be realized, as you can see in Listing 3-20.

Listing 3-20. Realizing Resources

```
realize User[james]
realize(Group[admin], Group[mainframe])
```

Here with the realize function we've realized the user resource james and the group resources admin and mainframe. You can see we've specified multiple resources to be realized by separating them with commas and enclosing them in brackets.

Note ➡ There is another variety of virtual resource called *exported resources*. Exported resources are virtual resources but are also exported to other hosts on your network. Exported resources are identified by the resource type prefixed by two @@ symbols rather than one. Exported resources are still experimental at this stage, so I am not going to address them, but you can read about them at http://www.reductivelabs.com/trac/puppet/wiki/VirtualResources.

Facts

Through this chapter, I've mentioned facts and Facter. Facter and Puppet are closely tied together. Puppet allows you to define and specify configuration to be applied to your nodes. Facter allows to you add information from your nodes to your Puppet configurations; for example, knowing the operating system of the node being configured allows you to customize a configuration resource for that platform (we used Facter in this manner in Listing 3-13 to select the appropriate name for a service depending on the operating system on the node).

Facts are available as variables defined in the top-level scope of your manifests. As we've seen earlier in this chapter, the value of the fqdn fact would be available as variable $fqdn. You can see the available facts about a particular system by executing the facter binary on the command line. A full list of facts and their values will be returned. This list will only contain the variables able to be returned on that particular platform. In Table 3-1, I've listed some of the facts commonly returned on platforms.

Table 3-1. Common Facts

Fact	Description
architecture	The architecture of the node, x86_64, for example
domain	The domain name of the node
facterversion	The version of Facter running on the node
fqdn	The fully qualified domain name of the node
hardwaremodel	The model of the hardware, for example, x86_64
hostname	The hostname of the node
id	The user running Facter
ipaddress	The IP address
kernel	The kernel type on the node

(Continued)

Turnbull

Fact	Description
kernelrelease	The kernel release of the kernel running on node
lsbdistcodename	The LSB codename of the distribution running on the node
lsbdistdescription	The LSB description of the distribution running on the node
lsbdistid	The LSB release ID of the distribution running on the node
lsbdistrelease	The LSB release number of the distribution running on node
macaddress	The MAC address of the node
memoryfree	The available memory
memorysize	The total memory size
operatingsystem	The node's operating system, for example, Fedora
operatingsystemrelease	The release of the node's operating system
processorx	The make of each processor, includes an entry for each processor, incremented from 0
processorcount	The total processor count
puppetversion	The version of Puppet on the node
rubyversion	The version of Ruby on the node
sshdsakey	The node's public DSA key
sshrsakey	The node's public RSA key
swapfree	The available swap space
swapsize	The total swap size

Tip ➡ On the Puppet master server, you also have access to other facts. The servername and serverip facts are the most useful, and these return the fully qualified domain name and IP address of the server, respectively.

Turnbull

Facter can also return environmental variables as facts. Facter assumes any environmental variable that is prefixed with FACTER_ is a fact that can be used by Puppet. So to set up one of these facts, we would simply configure an environmental variable as you can see in Listing 3-21.

Listing 3-21. Setting an Environmental Variable Fact

```
# export FACTER_statevar="primary"
```

In a Puppet manifest, we could then refer to the value of this environmental value using a variable just like any other Facter fact. In this case, the $statevar variable would contain a value of primary.

So what happens when the value of a fact changes? Puppet doesn't ignore this. As we described in Chapter 2, by default the client wakes up every 30 minutes and checks the currency of its configuration. When this check occurs, it does two things:

- Checks that no facts have changed on the node

- Checks that the modification time on the server-side configuration is earlier than the compilation time

If facts have changed, or the configuration on the master has been edited after the last compilation time, the client requests that the server recompile and redeliver the configuration. The client then reimplements and applies the updated configuration locally.

This check for fact changes does not apply to all facts though. Some facts are dynamic, such as memory and swap sizes, and the fact change check ignores these rather than initiating a recompile. By default, the following facts are ignored by the Puppet client:

- memorysize

- memoryfree

- swapsize

- swapfree

The list of facts to be ignored is controlled from the Puppet configuration file in the [puppetd] namespace and through the dynamicfacts configuration option.

```
dynamicfacts = memorysize,memoryfree,swapsize,swapfree
```

You can add further facts to be ignored by separating each fact with a comma.

Tip ➡ In Chapter 7, you'll see how to enhance Facter by adding your own facts for Puppet to use.

Resource Types

In this chapter, we've seen a few examples of the various resource types that can be used to manage resources on our nodes. We saw the file type resource that can manage files and directories, the service type that manages services and daemons, the group type that manages groups, and the package type that provides package management for our nodes. But these are not the only resource types available to us. There is a rich collection of resource types that we can make use of to configure resources on our nodes. It is also a collection that is growing rapidly as the developers and members of the community contribute new types. You can see the full list of resource types, their attributes, and examples of their functionality at http://reductivelabs.com/trac/puppet/wiki/ TypeReference.

Note ➡ In Chapter 7, I'll also discuss how you can use Ruby to create your own resource types and further enhance Puppet.

In Table 3-2, you can see a full list of the current resource types available at the time of writing.

Table 3-2. Resource Types

Resource Type	Description
cron	Manages cron jobs
exec	Executes external scripts
file	Manages files
filebucket	A repository for backing up files

(Continued)

Resource Type	Description
group	Manages groups
host	Manages host entries
interface	Configures interfaces (currently only works on Red Hat and Solaris)
mailalias	Manages mail aliases
maillist	Manages mailing lists
mount	Manages mount entries
notify	Sends a message to the puppetd log file
package	Manages packages
schedule	Defines Puppet scheduling
service	Manages services
sshkey	Manages SSH host keys
tidy	Removes unwanted files
user	Manages users
yumrepo	Manages YUM repositories
zones	Manages Solaris zones

Let's look at a selection of the resource types in Table 3-2 and how to make use of them.

Managing Cron Jobs

The first item in the table is the cron resource type that manages cron jobs on your nodes. You can see a cron resource in Listing 3-22.

Listing 3-22. cron *Resources*

```
cron { "syscheck":
        command => "/usr/bin/syscheck",
        user    => "root",
        hour    => "18",
        minute  => "0"
}
```

The cron resource type is very simple. The command attribute specifies the function, command, or binary that the cron job will execute. The user attribute specifies the user to run the cron job as, and the resource also supports the standard minutes, hours, days, months attributes that cron jobs use for scheduling.

Using a Filebucket

The filebucket type provides a repository for file backups. At this stage, the filebucket type allows you to specify a local or network repository to hold file backups for other resource types, principally the file resource type.

Files are backed up to the filebucket when they are changed on a client. Each change is assigned an MD5 checksum. This checksum can be used to later retrieve and restore files. At the moment, this is a manual restore process, but future plans are to automate this process so that the filebucket can aid in the transaction rollback process. Most sites define a single filebucket as their default backup location.

Note ➡ Puppet creates a local filebucket (called the clientbucket) on the local client and automatically backs up all files there. The filebucket resource is used to create a server-based version of this backup facility.

Defining a filebucket is easy as you can see on the following line:

```
filebucket { main: server => "puppetmaster.testing.com" }
```

The filebucket is created on the Puppet master server you specify with the server attribute.

Tip ➡ You can also create local filebuckets on clients by using the `path` attribute instead of the `server` attribute.

You can then refer to the created filebucket in resource types that support file backups, usually using the backup attribute. For example, you could specify a resource default that uses this filebucket to ensure all file resources use the filebucket to back up files:

```
File { backup => main }
```

You can see we've specified the capitalized `file` resource type to indicate this is a default and then the backup attribute. The backup attribute takes the name of a filebucket as a value. From now on, when a file is changed on a client, a backup will be saved to the `main` filebucket located on the Puppet master server.

Managing Host Files

The host resource manages the contents of host files on your nodes, usually /etc/hosts, but the type also supports adding host entries on OS X using NetInfo. You can see the `host` type in Listing 3-23.

Listing 3-23. The host *Type*

```
host { "router":
      ensure => present,
      ip      => "10.0.0.1",
      alias   => ["router.testing.com", "firewall"]
}
```

The type has a number of attributes, and we've shown some of them in Listing 3-23. The ensure attribute specifies whether the host entry should be added or deleted. The setting of present has Puppet add the host entry. A setting of absent would remove the entry. You can then specify the IP address using the `ip` attribute; you can specify either IPv4 or IPv6 addresses here. Last, we have the `alias` attribute, which allows you to list all the potential host aliases for the entry. Multiple entries must be specified with an array as shown in Listing 3-23. So this host resource would create a line in your hosts file like so:

```
10.0.0.1   router   router.testing.com   firewall
```

Managing SSH Host Keys

The sshkey resource type manages SSH host keys. The current resource type can be used to install keys in the known hosts file for your SSH server, /etc/ssh/ssh_known_hosts. You can see an sshkey resource type in Listing 3-24.

Listing 3-24. The sshkey *Resource Type*

```
sshkey { $hostname:
     type => dsa,
     key  => $sshdsakey
}
```

In Listing 3-24, we've used the sshkey resource together with two facts. We specified the title of the resource as the $hostname fact and the value of the key as the $sshdsakey fact. So what will Listing 3-23's resource do? For every node it is implemented on, it will place that node's DSA host key in the /etc/ssh/ssh_known_hosts file. We could also pass in a list of known host keys (using either DSA or RSA keys) or use the ensure attribute to indicate whether the key should be present or absent.

Tidy Unwanted Files

The tidy resource type is used to remove unwanted files based on certain criteria. You can specify criteria like the size or age of a file. In Listing 3-25, you can see a tidy resource.

Listing 3-25. The tidy *Resource Type*

```
tidy { "outputs":
     path   => "/tmp/dboutput.sql",
     age    => '15m',
     before => Service[mysql]
}
```

Listing 3-25 shows a tidy resource that will tidy (delete) the file /tmp/dboutput.sql if it is older than 15 minutes. We've given the resource the symbolic name of outputs and specified the precise file to be deleted using the path attribute. This is tidy's equivalent of using the name attribute.

The age is specified using the age attribute that can measure age in terms of seconds, minutes, hours, days, and weeks. The age is specified with a number and the first letter of the time period, for example, 1s for one second and 2d for two days. By default, the tidy resource uses atime, access time, to determine the age of a file, but you can override this to use ctime or mtime by specifying the type attribute like so:

```
type => "ctime"
```

In Listing 3-25, we have also used a new metaparameter, before. The before metaparameter is the opposite of the require metaparameter. The require metaparameter enforces dependency—another resource must be actioned prior to the current resource being actioned. The before metaparameter ensures that the current resource is actioned before the specified resource. In Listing 3-25, the outputs resource would have to be actioned before the Service[mysql] resource.

With the tidy resource, you can also remove files larger than a certain size by using the size attribute like so:

```
size => "10m"
```

You can specify size by bytes, kilobytes, or megabytes using b, k, and m, respectively, or if you don't specify a type, the resource will default to kilobytes.

If you specify both a size and an age, they are combined together as if with an OR statement. So if you specify a file to be tidied if it is older than 15 minutes or bigger than 1 megabyte, and the file fits one or both criteria, it will be tidied.

You can also back up files before they are tidied and recurse through directories to delete multiple files.

Tip ➡ You can see a full list of types and their attributes at
http://reductivelabs.com/trac/puppet/wiki/TypeReference.

Functions

Functions are the last part of Puppet's language we're going to examine. Functions come in two forms: *statements*, which do not return values, and *rvalues*, which do return values. You've already met two of these functions in this chapter: the include statement we used in our node definitions to include classes, and the realize function we use to realize virtual resources. Statements are used to perform jobs, like including classes or logging messages to the server, from which we don't expect a response. The rvalue functions return values and can only be used when a resulting value is expected such as a conditional statement or a variable assignment.

Tip ➡ Functions only run on the Puppet master. They are executed when the configuration on the master is parsed and compiled. So when you execute functions, you only have access to the resources on the master plus any Facter facts gathered from your nodes.

You can see a list of the currently available functions in Table 3-3.

Table 3-3. List of Functions

Function	Type	Description
include	Statement	Evaluates one or more classes
realize	Statement	Makes a virtual object real
alert	Statement	Logs a message on the server at level alert
crit	Statement	Logs a message on the server at level crit
debug	Statement	Logs a message on the server at level debug
emerg	Statement	Logs a message on the server at level emerg
err	Statement	Logs a message on the server at level err
info	Statement	Logs a message on the server at level info
notice	Statement	Logs a message on the server at level notice
warning	Statement	Logs a message on the server at level warning
defined	Rvalue	Determines whether a resource or class is defined
fail	Statement	Fails with a parse error
file	Rvalue	Returns the contents of a file or files
generate	Rvalue	Calls an external command and returns the results of the command

(Continued)

Function	Type	Description
search	Statement	Adds another namespace for this class to search
tag	Statement	Adds tags to a class, node, or definition
tagged	Rvalue	A Boolean function that tells you whether the current container is tagged with the specified tags
template	Rvalue	Evaluates templates and returns their values

The first two functions in Table 3-3, include and realize, we've already looked at earlier in this chapter.

Logging Functions

The functions alert, crit, debug, emerg, error, info, notice, and warning allow you to send messages to the Puppet master server. Each log level is a separate function, so to send a message to the server at the notice level, you would use the notice function like so:

```
notice("This is log message sent at notice log level")
```

Checking for Existence with defined

The next function, defined, ascertains whether a given resource or class is defined. You could use this to determine whether a class exists before including it, as you can see in Listing 3-26.

Listing 3-26. The defined Function

```
if defined(webservices) {
        include apache
} else {
        include lighttpd
}
```

In Listing 3-26, if the webservices class is defined, the apache class should be included. If not, the lighttpd class is included.

Note ➡ You'll note we've just specified the name of the class, rather than prefixing it with its proper title, `Class[classname]`. This is the behavior in version 0.23.2. Later versions refer to classes using the correct title (i.e., `if defined(Class[webservices]) { ... }`).

You can also use the `defined` function to check whether a resource is defined:

```
if defined(Service[sshd]) { ... }
```

Here we would perform an action if the `sshd` service is defined.

Note ➡ Like qualified variables, the `defined` function relies on the order that your resources are evaluated. If a resource hasn't been evaluated yet, you can't test its definition.

Generating Errors with fail

The `fail` function forces a parse error in your code and returns an error message to the server. You can make use of it like so:

```
fail("This function will result in a parse error")
```

This will result in an error similar to the following line being generated on the server:

```
err: This function will result in a parse error at ➡
/etc/puppet/manifests/classes.pp:32
```

Adding External Data with file

The `file` function returns the contents of a specified file or files. You can use this function to populate the contents of file type resources as you can see in Listing 3-27.

Listing 3-27. The file *Function*

```
file { "resolv.conf":
        name => "/etc/resolv.conf",
        owner => "root",
        group => "root",
        content => file("/var/puppet/file/resolv.conf")
}
```

In Listing 3-27, we have created a new file resource and then set its owner and group. We've used the content attribute of the file resource type to provide the contents of our new file. Inside the content attribute, we've called the file function and populated the file with the contents of the /var/puppet/file/resolv.conf file (which would have to be located on the master server). We can also specify multiple files like so:

```
file(["/var/puppet/file/hosts", "/var/puppet/file/secondary_hosts"])
```

Using generate

The generate function calls an external command (optionally with arguments) and returns the result to Puppet. You can see a generate function in Listing 3-28.

Listing 3-28. The generate *Function*

```
$interfaces = generate("/sbin/ifconfig", "eth0")
```

In Listing 3-28, we've defined a variable called $interfaces that calls the generate function. All generate functions must have a command specified, and then any potential arguments are specified after the command, each separated by commas. In Listing 3-28, the result of running the command

```
# /sbin/ifconfig eth0
```

would be returned to Puppet and used to populate the $interfaces variable. The command that executes must exit with a return code of 0. Any other return code will result in a parse error being generated.

Tip ➡ The generate function will only accept file separators, alphanumeric characters, dashes, and periods. There is some limited protection against malicious calls, but you should be careful when crafting your generate calls.

Qualifying Definitions Using search

The search function allows you to reference definitions contained in other classes without the need to qualify them. Remember how we discussed definition qualification? We discovered that we could refer to a definition defined in another class by specifying the class name and the definition name separated by two colons, ::. The search function allows you to add a "search path" to a class that allows referencing of definitions without qualification, for example:

```
class rails {
        define site { ... }
}

class webserver {
        search("rails")
        site { mysite: ... }
}
```

Here we've defined two classes, rails and webserver, and then created a definition called site in the rails class. We want to refer to this definition in the second class, and so we've added the search function and the name of the class that contains the definition we want to reference, in this case rails. We've then called the site definition.

Tip ➡ If we didn't use the search function, we could still refer to the site definition by using the syntax rails::site.

Using tag and tagged

The next two functions, tag and tagged, can be added to nodes, classes, and definitions to provide another method of classifying them.

Tip ➡ There is a metaparameter, also called tags, that can be used to tag individual resources.

Tagging allows you to group resources together, for example, specifying resources as belonging to a test or development environment. You can add as many tags as you wish.

Note ➡ Like other functions, tags are order dependent and set as resources are evaluated. You can't make use of a tag that has not been set yet.

```
node 'node.testing.com' {
      tag(devel)

      if tagged(devel) {
            include dev_test
      }
      include basics
}
```

On the previous lines, we've specified a node definition and used the `tag` function to add the `devel` tag. We've then used a conditional `if` clause and the `tagged` function. If the `devel` tag is applied to that node, the `dev_test` class will be included.

Some tags are automatically created; for example, all resources defined in a class, node, or definition structure will be tagged with the name of that structure. For example, if we define a file resource, /etc/passwd, in a class called `basics`, this resource would automatically have the tag `basics` added to it. Another example occurs when a class is included in a node; a tag with the same name as the class will then be set for that node. You can see how this might be useful in Listing 3-29.

Listing 3-29. Automatic Tagging

```
node 'node1.testing.com' {
      include webserver
      include basics
}

node 'node2.testing.com' {
      include databaseserver
      include basics
}

class basics {
      if tagged(webserver) {
            notice("This is a web server")
```

```
     }
     if tagged(databaseserver) {
             notice("This is a database server")
     }
}
```

In Listing 3-29, we create two nodes, node1, which includes the webserver and basics classes, and node2, which includes the databaseserver and basics classes.

We then define the basics class. Inside this class we use a combination of the if conditional and the tagged function. In this example, if the node including the basics class is tagged as webserver (which node1 automatically is as a result of including the webserver class), a notice is sent. If the node is tagged with databaseserver (as node2 is automatically), an alternative notice is sent.

Tip ➡ We can obviously do more than send a notice here, like implement a particular resource or load a particular package or packages.

We can also select which configuration is implemented based on tags. We do this in the Puppet configuration file by setting the value of the tags configuration option like so:

```
[puppetd]
tags = devel
```

Or, we can do so when Puppet is executed:

```
# puppetd --tags devel
```

The command on the previous line would execute Puppet and only implement configuration that was tagged devel. Multiple tags can be specified, separated by commas.

Using Templating

The last function, template, is also one of the most useful and allows you to make use of Ruby ERB templates. This allows us to create template files, like configuration files for example, that can be populated with configuration data from Puppet.

Tip ➡ With ERB, Ruby code is added to plain text to generate files. You can read about ERB templates in more detail at `http://www.ruby-doc.org/stdlib/libdoc/erb/rdoc/`.

In Listing 3-30, we can see a simple template.

Listing 3-30. Simple Template

```
class resolv {

        $searchpath = "testing.com"
        $nameservers = ["192.168.0.1", "192.168.0.2"]

        file { "resolv.conf":
                name => "/etc/resolv.conf",
                content => template("resolv-template.erb")
        }
}
```

In Listing 3-30, we've created a class called resolv and specified two variables, $searchpath and $nameservers (which is an array), and a file resource that configures the /etc/resolv.conf file. We've specified the content attribute and called the template function in it. We've specified a template file called resolv-template.erb.

Tip ➡ You can specify multiple templates by separating each with commas.

Template files need to be located on the master server, and by default, if you don't specify a full path, Puppet searches for them in the location specified in the templatedir configuration value in your configuration file. This option is usually set to /var/puppet/templates.

Inside a template you can reference any variable that is in the current scope; in Listing 3-30 you could use the $searchpath and $nameservers variables in the specified template. Now let's have a look at the template file.

```
search <%= searchpath %>
<% nameservers.each do |ns| %>nameserver <%= ns %>
<% end %>
```

You can see we've specified an ERB template that will receive the $searchpath and $nameservers variables. We've also specified a little piece of Ruby code that will iterate through the $nameservers array. Iteration can be used in conjunction with definitions to create multiple files of a particular type, for example, creating Apache virtual hosts. If we configure Listing 3-30 on a node, the end result would look like the following:

```
search testing.com
nameserver 192.168.0.1
nameserver 192.168.0.2
```

This is a very simple example of using the template function, and we'll see others, including using templates in definitions to create configuration and similar files in Chapter 4.

Resources

We've looked at how the Puppet language works in this chapter, and there are useful resources and documentation online that can also help you learn more.

You can also log tickets and bug reports at Puppet's trac site by registering at http://reductivelabs.com/trac/puppet/register.

Web

- *Puppet language tutorial*:

    http://reductivelabs.com/trac/puppet/wiki/LanguageTutorial
- *Puppet type reference (including metaparameters)*:

    http://reductivelabs.com/trac/puppet/wiki/TypeReference
- *Puppet function reference*:

    http://reductivelabs.com/trac/puppet/wiki/FunctionReference
- *Puppet style guide*:

    http://reductivelabs.com/trac/puppet/wiki/StyleGuide

## CHAPTER 4

Using Puppet

In Chapter 3, we talked about the syntax of the Puppet language and how to use that syntax to express configuration. In this chapter, we're going to look at Puppet's capabilities and how to make use of that language to articulate actual configurations on your nodes. We're going to do this by showing you how to configure a real environment using Puppet. Using the examples in this chapter, you will make use of the syntax you learned in Chapter 3.

All of these examples represent one way of implementing Puppet in your environment. The examples are designed to give you an idea of how a production Puppet implementation could work. Some of the examples represent some best practice guidelines, but others are simply ideas about how you might go about using Puppet to articulate your configuration.

We'll also look at how to manage and store your Puppet configuration including using a revision control system, file serving, and modules. By the end of this chapter, you should have a strong understanding of what Puppet can do to manage your nodes and the best way to articulate, store, and administer that configuration.

Note ➡ All the configuration examples in this chapter are available as a source code download from the Apress site.

Our Example Environment

We're going to configure an example environment with Puppet. You can see a visual representation of this environment in Figure 4-1.

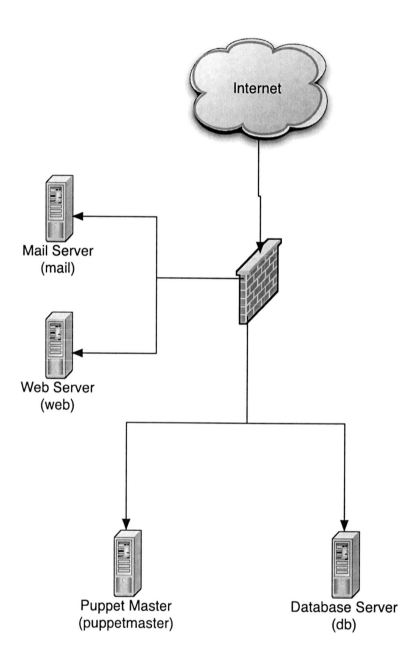

Figure 4-1. The example environment

The environment consists of four hosts running a variety of operating systems and with a variety of purposes. While four hosts may not seem like a lot, you'll see that the practices and structure I am going to demonstrate in this chapter can easily be extended to cater to larger numbers and types of hosts. You can see a full list of these hosts and their details in Table 4-1.

Table 4-1. Example Hosts

Host	Operating System	Description
web	Fedora	An Apache-based web server
db	Fedora	A MySQL-based database server
mail	Fedora	A Postfix-based mail server
puppetmaster	Debian	The Puppet master server

We've installed the latest version of Puppet on the puppetmaster host and the Puppet daemon on all the remote hosts. We've also connected our clients to the master and added them to the master using the puppetca binary. Our clients and master are installed with the default configuration.

Manifest Organization

Before we get started configuring our environment, we need to look at how Puppet manages and stores our configuration. As you'll remember, our resources, classes, and definitions are stored in manifest files. A special manifest file, called the site manifest, is at the core of our configuration. When starting the Puppet master daemon, the site manifest file, by default located in /etc/puppet/manifests/site.pp, needs to be present and syntactically correct.

Importing Manifests

If we added all our configuration to the site.pp file, it'd quickly become complicated and hard to manage. So instead, we store our configuration in multiple files. We think about the site manifest file as the apex of a pyramid; in this file, all other manifests and the configuration defined in them must be referenced. This is done by importing files into your site manifest file. We do this using the import function as you can see in Listing 4-1.

Listing 4-1. The import *Function*

```
import "templates.pp"
import "nodes.pp"
import "classes/*"
import "groups/*"
import "users/*"
import "os/*"
```

In Listing 4-1, we've used five import statements. First, we've imported the file templates.pp and the file nodes.pp. You do not have to specify the .pp extension. By default, Puppet will add the .pp extension to any file specified in the import statement that doesn't already have it. Next, we've used globbing to import the contents of three subdirectories: groups, users, and os.[1] By specifying the * symbol, Puppet will load all of the files that have an extension of .pp in those directories.

We also might use our site.pp file to set up a default filebucket or some other defaults for types as we have in Listing 4-2.

Listing 4-2. Other Items in the site.pp *File*

```
filebucket { main: server => puppet }
File { backup => main }
```

In Listing 4-2, we've defined a default filebucket and told the file type to always back up files to that filebucket.

We can also apply a structure to the files we import into our site.pp file. In Table 4-2, I've shown an example structure of files and directories to hold your configuration resources.

---

[1] http://www.faqs.org/docs/abs/HTML/globbingref.html

Table 4-2. Manifest Structure

Structure	Description
/manifests/	The manifest root directory
/manifests/site.pp	The primary manifest file
/manifests/templates.pp	Contains template nodes
/manifests/nodes.pp	Contains node definitions
/manifests/definitions/	Houses all definitions
/manifests/groups/	Contains manifests configuring groups
/manifests/os/	Contains classes designed to configure nodes with particularoperating systems
/manifests/users/	Contains manifests configuring users
/manifest/files/	Contains file server modules for Puppet distributable files
/manifests/templates/*classname*	ERB templates contained in subdirectories named after the class that uses the template

We'll discuss and expand on the structure in Table 4-2 further during this chapter. You can locate this directory structure wherever it suits you. By default, Puppet looks for the manifest files in /etc/puppet/manifests, controlled by the manifestdir configuration option.

manifestdir = $confdir/manifests

Other people locate their manifests under the /var/puppet directory. You should choose the location that best suits your environment and standards. We can also override and change the name of the site.pp file using the manifest configuration option:

manifest = $manifestdir/site.pp

The manifest option defaults to the value of $manifestdir/site.pp.

Managing Manifests with Subversion

One last manifest management tool we're going to use is a version control system, which is the best tool for managing a large number of manifests. We're going to use a Subversion repository. *Subversion* is an open source version control system that can store and manage your manifest files. Subversion manages files and directories and tracks changes made to them over time. This allows you to revert changes or restore to a previous state. To use Subversion, you will need to install it. Most Linux and Unix hosts will have a Subversion package available; for example, on a Debian platform, you would need to install the subversion package.

Note ➡ If you don't like or use Subversion as a version control tool, you can use an alternative tool like Git, Monotone, or CVS.

First, we create a Subversion repository.

```
$ svnadmin create /usr/local/svn/puppet
```

Next, in Listing 4-3, we add our Puppet directory structure and files to the repository.

Listing 4-3. Subversion Import

```
$ svn import puppet file:///usr/local/svn/puppet ➡
-m "Initial import of Puppet structure"
Adding          puppet/site.pp
Adding          puppet/template.pp
Adding          puppet/nodes.pp
...
Committed revision 1.
```

In Listing 4-3, we've imported the contents of the puppet directory into the repository we created. You can see each file being added and the final message indicating that the first revision has been committed to the repository. If we now wish to check out these files into what Subversion calls a "working copy" to use in Puppet, we can do this using the svn checkout function.

```
$ svn checkout file:///usr/local/svn/puppet /etc/puppet/manifests
```

We then make any updates and changes to our working directory. Then each time we update our Puppet manifests, we commit our changes using the svn commit command.

```
$ cd /etc/puppet/manifests
$ svn commit -m "Added firewall node"
```

We can now potentially revert back to a previous revision of our configuration if we wish to reverse a change or changes.

Tip ➡ If you've never used Subversion before, an excellent introduction is available at `http://svnbook.red-bean.com/`. You can also see details of the various Subversion options by running the `svn` command with the help option: `svn help`.

Defining Nodes

Let's configure our nodes first. We'll start with the node definitions themselves, and to make it easier, we're going to classify our nodes into types and build some templates. We're going to template our nodes on the assumption that we're going to have multiple mail, web, firewall, and database hosts in our environment. So we're going to create a base node and some template nodes for each.

Caution ➡ As I mentioned in Chapter 3, template nodes (and node inheritance) is generally only useful for inheriting and templating nodes with static classes that do not include variables. Say we want to specify a variable in our node that overrides a particular variable in a template node; unfortunately, due to variable scope, we can't. We discussed this limitation in Chapter 3. Later in this section, you'll see another method using the `include` function workaround we also discussed in Chapter 3.

We're going to place these templates in a file called `templates.pp`, shown in Listing 4-4, and we'll need to update our `site.pp` file to import this file.

Listing 4-4. `templates.pp`

```
node basenode {
        case $operatingsystem {
                fedora: { include fedora }
                debian: { include debian }
                default: { include fedora}
        }
        include baseapps, sshd
}
node default inherits basenode {}
node webserver inherits basenode {
        include apache
}
```

```
node dbserver inherits basenode {
        include mysql
}
node mailserver inherits basenode {
        include postfix
}
```

In Listing 4-4, we've created our template nodes. The first, basenode, is configuration we're going to apply to all nodes. In our basenode we've made use of a fact, $operatingsystem, to include a class based on the operating system of the node; for example, if Facter returned a value of fedora, the fedora class would be included.

We've then defined a default node, which inherits basenode. The default node is applied to any nodes that do not have specific node definitions. We've then created three templates, webserver, dbserver, and mailserver, which all inherit basenode and add classes of their own. At this stage, we've just included a small number of classes into each template.

There is an alternative method of inheriting classes between parent and child nodes that uses the include function. This method is better suited to classes where variable scoping and inheritance is an issue. You can see an example of that method next:

```
class baseclass {
        case $operatingsystem {
                fedora: { include fedora }
                debian: { include debian }
                default: { include fedora}
        }
        include baseapps, sshd
}
node default {
        include baseclass
}
class webserver {
        include baseclass
        include apache
}
class dbserver {
        include baseclass
        include mysql
}
class mailserver {
        include baseclass
        include postfix
}
```

In this alternative method, we've defined a class called `baseclass` rather than a base node. This class is then included in all subsequent classes including the `default` node. Additional classes are created that contain the base class and classes required to template other nodes much as we did in Listing 4-4.

Now let's add node definitions for the actual nodes we're going to manage. We're going to create a file called `nodes.pp` to store them and import that into our `site.pp` file (as you can see in Listing 4-5).

Listing 4-5. `nodes.pp`

```
node 'puppetmaster.testing.com' inherits basenode {}
node 'web.testing.com' inherits webserver {}
node 'db.testing.com' inherits dbserver {}
node 'mail.testing.com' inherits mailserver {}
```

Note ➡ You can also store node definitions external to Puppet in an LDAP directory. You can read about that at `http://reductivelabs.com/trac/puppet/wiki/LdapNodes`. We'll discuss this further in Chapter 6.

In our `nodes.pp` file, we've created a node definition for each node we're going to manage. We've specified each node by its fully qualified domain name and enclosed the name in single quotes. We haven't added any specific classes to the node definitions and are just inheriting the templates we created in Listing 4-4.

Note ➡ Remember, nodes can only inherit one node.

If we wanted to add multiple nodes of each template, we could add them in a list, each separated by commas, like so:

```
node 'web.testing.com', 'web1.testing.com', 'web2.testing.com' inherits webserver
{}
```

If we used our alternative `include` method, we'd create our nodes like so:

```
node 'puppetmaster.testing.com' {
    include baseclass
}
node 'web.testing.com' {
```

```
        include webserver
}
node 'db.testing.com' {
        include dbserver
}
node 'mail.testing.com' {
        include mailserver
}
```

Again, if we wanted to apply our template classes to multiple nodes, we'd do it like so:

```
node 'web.testing.com', 'web1.testing.com', 'web2.testing.com' {
        include webserver
}
```

Our First Classes

As we defined our nodes, we also referenced our first classes. Let's create those classes now. We're going to create all our classes in a directory called `classes` under our `manifest` directory and import all of them into our configuration in our `site.pp` file (again, as we've already seen in Listing 4-1). I generally create each class in a separate file and giving the file the same name as the class itself, for example, `baseapps.pp` for the `baseapps` class. We then specify in our `site.pp` that Puppet should import the files in the `classes` directory.

```
import "classes/*"
```

The previous `import` statement will import all files with an extension of `.pp` in the classes directory.

In Listing 4-4, you can see that the basenode class includes two classes, `baseapps` and `sshd`, in addition to including a class based on the operating system of the node we're managing, in this case the `debian` and `fedora` classes. In Listing 4-6, you can see our first two classes: `baseapps` and `sshd`.

Listing 4-6. baseapps *Class*

```
class baseapps {

        $packagelist = ["joe", "perl", "rubygems"]

        package { $packagelist:
                ensure => installed }
}
```

```
class sshd {

case $operatingsystem {
        fedora: { $ssh_packages = ["openssh", "openssh-server", "openssh-clients"] }
        debian: { $ssh_packages = ["openssh-server", "openssh-client"] }
        default: { $ssh_packages = ["openssh", "openssh-server"] }
}

        package { $ssh_packages: ensure => installed }

        service { sshd:
                name => $operatingsystem ? {
                    fedora => "sshd",
                    debian => "ssh",
                    default => "sshd",
                    },
                enable => true,
                ensure => running
        }

}
```

Tip ➡ To help with your manifest creation and editing, there is a VIM syntax validation file, `puppet.vim`, available at `http://reductivelabs.com/downloads/puppet/puppet.vim`.

Our first two classes are simple. The baseapps class defines an array holding a number of packages: the joe editor, which my system administrators prefer, `perl` for our system administration scripts, and the `rubygems` Ruby package manager. This array is then added to the package type that will then install each package. The providers associated with the package type will then use each node's package management system to install the packages, for example, `apt-get` on Debian and `yum` on Fedora.

When we apply our class to each node, the packages will be installed if they are not already present. If a package needs to be installed, you'll see a log message indicating its change in status:

```
notice: //basenode/baseapps/Package[joe]/ensure: ensure changed ➡
'purged' to 'present'
```

The second class, sshd, sets up the SSH daemon on all our nodes. The first resource ensures that, depending on the operating system on the node, the appropriate packages are installed. The second resource, Service[sshd], ensures that the SSH daemon is started. It uses the name attribute and a conditional statement to ensure the right service is started on each operating system.

We also defined two other classes, debian and fedora, which are loaded for the respective operating system. We're going to put these classes into the os directory and also import them into our site.pp file (again, we've already seen this in Listing 4-1).

```
import "os/*"
```

In Listing 4-7, you can see both these classes.

Listing 4-7. The Operating System Classes

```
class fedora {

    yumrepo { "testing.com-repo":
        baseurl => "http://repos.testing.com/fedora/$lsbdistrelease/",
        descr => "Testing.com's YUM repository",
        enabled => 1,
        gpgcheck => 0,
    }
}

class debian {

    $disableservices = ["hplip", "avahi-daemon", "rsync", "spamassassin"]

    service { $disableservices:
        enable => false,
        ensure => stopped,
    }
}
```

In Listing 4-7, we've created two classes; the first is fedora, which loads whenever a node returns Fedora as the value of the $operatingsystem fact. It uses the yumrepo type to setup a yum repository for our environment. We've also used another fact, $lsbdistrelease, which returns the LSB release number to select the correct repository for the Fedora release we have installed.

On the following line, you can see the log entry indicating that the repository has been created:

```
info: create new repo testing.com-repo in file ➡
/etc/yum.repos.d/testing.com-repo.repo
```

The resulting repository will be created on your node.

```
[testing.com-repo]
name=Testing.com's YUM repository
baseurl=http://repos.testing.com/fedora/7/
enabled=1
gpgcheck=0
```

The second class, `debian`, loads when Debian nodes connect, and it uses the `service` type to disable an array of services that we don't want running on our Debian hosts.

We could create and load classes for other operating systems and platforms or additional types to the operating system classes we've already created.

Managing Users and Groups

Once we've created our nodes, we're going to create some users and groups for our nodes. Puppet recommends that all users and groups be created as virtual resources and realized. We discussed virtual resources in Chapter 3 and why we use them. Virtual resources are not automatically configured on your nodes, but rather require explicit application. You can recognize virtual resources by the @ symbol preceding the type.

Virtual resources are useful for users and groups. This is because a resource can only be managed once in Puppet. Hence we could not configure a user called `sysadmin` in both the `debian` and `fedora` classes. With virtual resources, we can create the `sysadmin` user as a virtual resource. We then realize the resource in both classes. We can do the same thing with groups.

Caution ➡ Puppet is probably not ideal to populate large numbers of users and groups to provide user access for nodes and applications. Puppet is best used to populate nodes with users for running applications and services, systems administration, and management.

We're going to define two types of users. The first are users associated with functions, such as our `sysadmin` user, or users belonging to employees and administrators. These users will be grouped into a single class called `virt_users` and contained in a file called `virt_users.pp`. The second are those used by appliances, services, and daemons. Each of these users will be specified in their own classes, and each class will be prefixed with user_ and the name of the user being created, for example, user_apache. Each user class will be specified in its own file.

We'll divide groups into the same types and use the same model to manage them. All groups associated with people will be contained in a class called virt_groups and in a file called virt_groups.pp. Groups for applications, services, and daemons will be contained in individual classes and prefixed with group_ and the name of the group being created, for example, group_apache. Each group will be specified in its own file.

Then we need to import both the users and groups directories to our site.pp file to ensure all our users and groups are loaded.

```
import "groups/*"
import "users/*"
```

Managing Users

In Listing 4-8, you can see part of our virt_users class, showing two of our users.

Listing 4-8. The virt_users *Class*

```
class virt_users {
        @user { "jsmith":
                ensure  => "present",
                uid     => "1001",
                gid     => "1000",
                comment => "Jane Smith",
                home    => "/nfs/IT/home/jsmith",
                shell   => "/bin/bash",
        }

        @user { "mjones":
                ensure  => "present",
                uid     => "1002",
                gid     => "1000",
                comment => "Mary Jones",
                home    => "/nfs/IT/home/mjones",
                shell   => "/bin/bash",

        }
}
```

Note ➡ When creating users, any group or groups you specify must exist, or the user creation will fail. Here we have used the group `administration`. This group must already exist on our target node, or a Puppet resource must exist that will create this group on the node.

With groups, we follow the same model. In Listing 4-9, you can see a selection from our `virt_groups` class that contains employee groups.

Listing 4-9. The `virt_groups` *Class*

```
class virt_groups {
        @group { "staff":
                gid     => "1000",
                ensure  => present
        }

        @group { "administration":
                gid     => "1501",
                ensure => present
        }

        @group { "mail_team":
                gid     => "1502",
                ensure => present
        }
}
```

So how do we realize these users and groups? Well, first we're going to realize the users and one of our groups in a class called `staff`, which we'll store in our `classes` directory with the file name `staff.pp`. We've also included the contents of our `virt_users` and `virt_groups` classes to ensure Puppet knows where to find our users and groups.

```
class staff {
        include virt_users, virt_groups
        realize(
                Group["staff"],
                User["jsmith"],
                User["mjones"]
        )
}
```

We can then include this class in our basenode template to ensure this group and its users are created on all nodes that inherit this template node.

```
node basenode {
     case $operatingsystem {
            fedora: { include fedora }
            debian: { include debian }
            default: { include fedora}
     }
     include baseapps, sshd, staff
}
```

But we also want our administration group to be included on all nodes. So in Listing 4-10, we're going to create a class called administrators to realize the administration group and add one of our users to that group. We'll store our class in a file called administrators.pp in our classes directory. We'll then include that class in our basenode node in the nodes.pp file.

Listing 4-10. Realizing Our Users

```
class administrators inherits virt_users {
     realize(
            Group["administration"]
     )
     User["jsmith"] { groups => "administration" }
}

node basenode {
     case $operatingsystem {
            fedora: { include fedora }
            debian: { include debian }
            default: { include fedora}
     }
     include baseapps, sshd, staff, administrators
}
```

You can see in Listing 4-10 that we've used an override to add the administration group to the jsmith user. To achieve the override, the administrators class inherits the virt_users class. Now, the administration group will be created on all templates and nodes that inherit the basenode node template and the jsmith user added as a member of this group.

We could also realize these users in other classes; for example, if mjones was a mail administrator, we could create a class for mail administrators, stored in classes/mail_team.pp, and include it in our mailserver template node like so:

Turnbull

```
class mail_team inherits virt_users {
        realize(
                Group["mail_team"]
        )
        User["mjones"] { groups => "mail_team" }
}

node mailserver inherits basenode {
        include postfix
        include mail_team
}
```

Here the `mail_team` group would be realized and included in the `mailserver` node template. We've again used an override to add the `mjones` user to the `mail_team` group. Now every node that uses this node template, in our case the `mail.testing.com` node, will add the `mjones` user to the `mail_team` group.

We can also create single users and groups for particular purposes, for example, a user and group to run a daemon or application. You can see an example of this in Listing 4-11.

Listing 4-11. The `mysql` User and Group

```
class mysql_user {
        user { "mysql":
        ensure  => "present",
        uid     => "501",
        gid     => "501",
        comment => "MySQL",
        home    => "/var/lib/mysql",
        shell   => "/sbin/nologin",
        }
}
class mysql_group {
        group { "mysql":
        gid     => "501",
        ensure => present
        }
}
```

We can then include both the user and the group when we configure the appropriate service. We don't make this user and group virtual, as we're only going to be using them in one class.

Tip ➡ There is a useful script available at the Reductive Labs site that can convert a passwd file into a class
containing all the users defined in the file. You can see the script at
http://reductivelabs.com/trac/puppet/wiki/PuppetBestPractice#conv-passwd.

File Serving

Before we configure the services on our nodes, we're going to look at how Puppet does file
serving. Puppet can act as a file server to deliver files to your nodes when required. The
files Puppet serves out via file servers are called *distributable files.*

File serving with Puppet has both a server and client function. The server function is
configured and initiated by the Puppet master daemon. The client function is embedded into
the Puppet client daemon and retrieves files from the Puppet master file server. The file
retrieval is done in individual resource definitions. You can specify a Puppet file server for
the file type resource using the source attribute like so:

```
file { "httpd.conf":
      source => "puppet://puppetmaster/httpd/conf/httpd.conf"
}
```

Let's start by configuring our file server. File server configuration is controlled by the
fileserver.conf file, by default located in the /etc/puppet directory. You can specify an
alternative location for the file by starting the Puppet master daemon with the --fsconfig
flag like so:

```
# puppetmasterd --fsconfig /usr/local/etc/puppet/fileserver.conf
```

The fileserver.conf file defines paths to serve files from and the access controls
around those paths. In Listing 4-12, you can see an example of a typical configuration.

Listing 4-12. fileserver.conf *Configuration*

```
[configuration]
path /etc/puppet/manifests/files/configuration
allow *.testing.com
deny *.production.com
```

Each path being served is called a *module.* Listing 4-12 shows a module called
configuration. The use of modules allows Puppet to abstract and simplify file system
configuration and paths. The path statement specifies the location on the Puppet master

server where the files being served are located. The path can contain one or more %h, %d, and %H dynamic variables. They are the client's hostname, domain name, and fully qualified domain name. All are based on the host and domain name used by the Puppet client's SSL certificate. This allows you to specify particular files to be downloaded based on these names, for example:

```
path /etc/puppet/manifests/files/%h
```

In this path statement, the %h variable would be replaced with the hostname of the connecting node and retrieve files from a directory named after that node like so:

```
/etc/puppet/manifests/files/web/filename
/etc/puppet/manifests/files/db/filename
/etc/puppet/manifests/files/mail/filename
```

There are also simple host- and IP-based access controls for file serving using an allow-and-deny model. In Listing 4-12, we've specified both an allow and a deny statement. We're allowing access to all nodes in the testing.com domain and denying access to all nodes in the production.com domain. In your Puppet master logs, when you start the daemon, you should see an informational message for each mount module you define like so:

```
info: mount[configuration]: allowing *.testing.com access
```

If you do not specify any deny or allow statements, file serving is explicitly denied. When working out whether a node has access, deny statements are processed and matched before allow statements. If, after processing all statements, no allow statements provide access to the module, the request is denied.

You can specify which nodes to allow or deny using a variety of formats: name, IP address, or the * symbol. You can see a few example statements on the following lines:

```
deny 10.0.10.0/24
deny dev.testing.com
deny 10.0.20.*
allow *
```

On the previous lines, we have denied access to the 10.0.10.0 Class C subnet, the host dev.testing.com, and all the hosts in the 10.0.20.x subnet. Lastly, we used the * symbol to specify a global allow.

Tip ➡ The file server function can be performance intensive and can result in performance impacts on the Puppet master server. This is particularly evident when you retrieve large numbers of files on multiple nodes. At this stage, there are limited solutions to this issue, but some discussions on scalability can be seen at http://www.reductivelabs.com/trac/puppet/wiki/PuppetScalability.

If we want to retrieve a file in the configuration module, we would use the file resource type as you can see in Listing 4-13.

Listing 4-13. Retrieving Served Files

```
file { "/etc/nsswitch.conf":
    source => "puppet://puppetmaster/configuration/nsswitch.conf"
}
```

In Listing 4-13, we've retrieved the nsswitch.conf file from our Puppet master server, here puppetmaster. The source attribute of the file type allows us to specify the location of the file to be retrieved. It takes the format of

```
puppet://server/module/file
```

In our listing, the server name is puppetmaster and the module is our previously defined configuration. We then specify the source file to be retrieved. If you omit the server value, for example, puppet:///module/file, Puppet will automatically try to fill in the value of the server name based on the Puppet master server that you are connecting to.

We can also download the contents of whole directories recursively using the recurse attribute like so:

```
file { "/etc/pam.d":
    source  => "puppet://puppetmaster/configuration/pam.d",
    recurse => "true"
}
```

Instead of specifying a file in the file resource type, we specify a directory. The source statement also specifies a directory located on our file server. The recurse attribute tells Puppet that all files contained in the source directory should be retrieved and downloaded to the target node.

Tip ➡ You can also copy from more than one source by specifying multiple entries in the source attribute. You can see details of how to do this in the Type Reference at http://reductivelabs.com/trac/puppet/wiki/TypeReference#file.

Modularizing Our Configuration

Now that we've configured the basics of our nodes and introduced user management and file serving, we need to add some services, like mail, databases, and web services, to our nodes. We're going to configure MySQL on our db.testing.com node, the Postfix mail server on our mail.testing.com node, and finally Apache on our www.testing.com node.

To add these services, we're going to use one of Puppet's more powerful features: modules. Modules are collections of configuration—manifests, templates, and files—that can be reused and distributed. For example, instead of creating individual classes for installing and managing MySQL, we're going to create a MySQL module.

So why use modules? Well, if the application, daemon, or function you are configuring contains multiple classes, files, and/or templates, the easiest way to package these resources is to modularize them. Modules make management of configuration collections easier and more structured.

Modules are structured very simply. They are stored under a directory specified in the modulepath configuration variable in the puppet.conf configuration file or on the command line using --modulepath. By default, these are the $confdir/modules (/etc/puppet/modules in most installations) and /usr/share/puppet/modules directories. We can also specify multiple module paths as colon-separated lists of directories like so:

```
modulepath $confdir/modules:/usr/share/puppet/modules: ➡
/usr/local/share/puppet/modules
```

Modules are then included into your configuration using the import function as you can see in Listing 4-14.

Listing 4-14. Importing Modules

```
import "mysql"
```

Tip ➡ From version 0.23.1, Puppet tries to automatically load classes and definitions contained in your module path. This means if you want to use a specific class or definition from your module in your configuration, you can simply include the class or start using the definition without needing to explicitly import the whole module.

So how does Puppet know what resources to load? Each module is defined using a directory structure and an initialization file called the init.pp file. Each module should have a minimum of the following directory structure:

```
module_path/
  module_name/
    module_name/manifests/
    module_name/manifests/init.pp
```

Tip ➡ It is often useful to put a README file in the root directory of the module that describes your module and its structure, files, and any dependencies.

The init.pp file, which is automatically processed when you import a module, should be located in the module_name/manifests directory. For example, if we had a module called mysql located in the default modules directory, Puppet would expect to find the init.pp file in the following location:

```
/etc/puppet/modules/mysql/manifests/init.pp
```

The init.pp file has a dual function. It can contain the core classes used in the module or provide a location from which to import the classes or definitions that make up the module. If you import additional classes or definitions, these should be located in directories underneath the manifests directory. An example of an init.pp file can be seen in Listing 4-15.

Listing 4-15. The init.pp *File*

```
class mysql {
        package { "mysql-server":
        ...
        }

        service { "mysqld":
        ...
        }
}
```

In Listing 4-15, we've defined a class called mysql in which we've configured sample package and service resources.

So when importing a module, for example, the mysql module, Puppet will look in all of the module paths for a directory called mysql. It will then check the manifests directory in the root of the mysql directory for the init.pp file and load the file and process its contents.

Puppet also allows some clever namespace manipulation to make using modules easier. By creating a module, we also create a namespace; for example, the mysql module would create a namespace called mysql. Using this namespace, we can easily define and refer to additional classes in our module. For example, let's say we want to add a new class to our mysql module called server. To do this, we would define a class called mysql::server and store it in a file called server.pp in the manifests directory of our mysql module. We can then use this module by simply including it like so:

```
include mysql::server
```

Puppet will recognize this namespace and find and load the class in the correct module directory and file.

This namespace magic also extends to templates and files. To make use of this, we can create two additional directories underneath the module root, called templates and files. These directories should contain any templates or files that are included in the module, respectively. Your templates can then be referenced by specifying the name of the module and the name of the template like so:

```
template("mysql/my.cnf.erb"}
```

Puppet will then automatically look in the correct module path for the templates directory and load the required template.

Files contained in your module can also be served out using Puppet's file server functionality. Each module automatically creates its own file serving module and loads any files stored in the files directory of your module. For example, in our mysql module, files can be served using the source attribute by employing the following structure:

```
source => "puppet://puppetmaster/mysql/my.cnf"
```

This will retrieve a file called my.cnf from the files directory of the mysql module.

In your fileserver.conf configuration file, there is also special file module mount called [modules] that can be defined. This mount allows you to control access to files contained in modules. This file module is defined without a path statement and restricts access to files contained in all modules. Currently, more granular controls, for example, on a per module basis, are not available.

Caution ➡ Modules automatically create their own file server modules, so you don't need to update your fileserver.conf file. But in your fileserver.conf file, you cannot have another file server module defined that has the same name as one of your configuration modules.

You can read more about modules and module organization at
http://www.reductivelabs.com/trac/puppet/wiki/PuppetModules and
http://reductivelabs.com/trac/puppet/wiki/ModuleOrganisation.

MySQL Module

Let's look at an example of our first module, mysql. We're going to locate it in the
/etc/puppet/modules directory and structure it like so:

```
/etc/puppet/modules/mysql
/etc/puppet/modules/mysql/manifests/init.pp
/etc/puppet/modules/mysql/files/my.cnf
```

We've included the required init.pp file and one other file, the my.cnf configuration
file, in our module. We're going to put most of our module's logic in the init.pp file, and
you can see that in Listing 4-16.

Listing 4-16. The mysql *Module's* init.pp

```
class mysql {

$packagelist = ["mysql", "mysql-server", "mysql-libs"]

package { $packagelist:
        ensure => installed }

file { "/etc/my.cnf":
        owner   => "root",
        group   => "root",
        mode    => "0644",
        replace => true,
        source  => "puppet:///mysql/my.cnf",
        require => Package["mysql-libs"]
}

service { mysqld:
        enable  => "true",
        ensure  => "running",
        require => File["/etc/my.cnf"]
}
}
```

In Listing 4-16, you can see our `mysql` module. It contains three resources. The first is a package resource that installs the three packages used for MySQL on our node. The second resource is a `file` type resource that retrieves the `my.cnf` configuration file from the master server. You'll note we've excluded the name of the master server from the `source` attribute, instead specifying `puppet:///`, which tells Puppet to insert the name of the server itself. The `file` resource also uses the `require` attribute to tell Puppet that the `mysql-libs` package must be loaded before the file is retrieved. The last resource is a service that starts the `mysqld` service. It also has a `require` attribute that specifies that the `File["/etc/my.cnf"]` resource must be processed prior to this resource.

In Listing 4-4, you'll also see that we included the `mysql` module in our `templates.pp` file as part of the `dbserver` template node.

Postfix Module

Our next module will install and manage a Postfix mail server. The structure of our Postfix module can be seen here:

```
/etc/puppet/modules/postfix
/etc/puppet/modules/postfix/manifests/init.pp
/etc/puppet/modules/postfix/manifests/postfix_files.pp
/etc/puppet/modules/postfix/files/aliases.db
/etc/puppet/modules/postfix/files/main.cf
/etc/puppet/modules/postfix/files/master.cf
```

We've specified an `init.pp` file, a definition, and three configuration files in the `postfix` module. Like the `mysql` module, we've included all required configuration in the `init.pp` file, barring a single definition that we've placed in the `postfix_files.pp` file. You can see the contents of the `init.pp` file in Listing 4-17.

Listing 4-17. The postfix *Module's* init.pp *File*

```
class postfix {

$mailadmin = "postmaster@$domain"

$packagelist = ["postfix.$architecture", "postfix-pflogsumm.$architecture"]

package { $packagelist:
        ensure => "installed"
}
```

```
postfix::postfix_files {

"/etc/aliases.db":
        mode   => "0640",
        source => "aliases.db";

"/etc/postfix/main.cf":
        source => "main.cf";

"/etc/postfix/master.cf":
        source => "master.cf"
}

service { "postfix":
        enable => "true",
        ensure => "running",
        require => Package["postfix.$architecture"]
}

cron { pflogsumm:
        hour   => 2,
        minute => 15,
        user   => mail,
        command => "/usr/sbin/pflogsumm -d yesterday /var/log/maillog | ➥
mail -s 'pflogsumm from $fqdn' $mailadmin",
        require => Package["postfix-pflogsumm.$architecture"]
}
}
```

In Listing 4-17, we've defined a class called postfix. Inside the class, we've defined a number of resources and two variables. The first variable, $mailadmin, defines the mail administrator for our nodes; it makes use of the $domain fact to populate this attribute. The second variable is an array of packages to be loaded. The package listing takes advantage of another fact, $architecture, to ensure that the right package for each node is loaded.

Then we've defined some resources to manage our Postfix configuration. We first install the postfix and postfix-pflogsumm packages. Next, we retrieve our three configuration files from our file server. To do this, we use the definition we've created. The definition is a shortcut that populates most of the required attributes for our file resource type. The postfix::postfix_files definition can be seen in Listing 4-18.

Listing 4-18. The `postfix::postfix_files` *Definition*

```
define postfix::postfix_files($owner = root, $group = root, $mode = 644, ➥
$source, $backup = false, $recurse = false, $ensure = file) {

    file { $name:
        mode    => $mode,
        owner   => $owner,
        group   => $group,
        backup  => $backup,
        recurse => $recurse,
        ensure  => $ensure,
        require => Package["postfix.$architecture"],
        source  => "puppet:///postfix/$source"
    }
}
```

The `postfix::postfix_files` definition is very simple. It specifies some defaults for each file specified to the definition, uses the `require` attribute to ensure the `postfix` package is installed prior to the file, and uses the value passed from the `source` attribute when the definition is invoked to specify where to retrieve the file from.

Then we enable and ensure that the Postfix services are started. Lastly, we add a cron job that enables `pflogsumm` reports to be generated and sent. We use the `$fqdn` fact and our `$mailadmin` variable in our cron job.

Note ➥ Throughout the module, we've also made use of the `require` attribute to ensure that all our resources are processed in a logical order.

Again, in Listing 4-4, you'll see that we have included the `postfix` module in our `templates.pp` file as part of the `mailserver` template node.

Apache Module

The last module we're going to create is the `apache` module that will install and manage the Apache web server. The structure of our Apache module can be seen here:

```
/etc/puppet/modules/apache
/etc/puppet/modules/apache/manifests/init.pp
/etc/puppet/modules/apache/manifests/virtual_host.pp
/etc/puppet/modules/apache/manifests/apache_files.pp
/etc/puppet/modules/apache/files/httpd.conf
/etc/puppet/modules/apache/templates/virtual_host.erb
```

We've defined an init.pp file; a file called virtual_host.pp, which contains a definition that will allow us to create virtual hosts; and the apache_files.pp file, which contains the apache::apache_files class that provides some file management shortcuts, much like the postfix::postfix_files class in the postfix module. We also create the httpd.conf configuration file in the files directory and finally a template for our virtual hosts in a file called virtual_host.erb in the templates directory.

Let's start by looking at the init.pp file that contains the core configuration for the module in Listing 4-19.

Listing 4-19. The apache *Module's* init.pp

```
class apache {

$packagelist = ["httpd", "webalizer", "mod_ssl"]

package { $packagelist:
        ensure => "installed"
}

apache::apache_files {

"/etc/httpd/conf/httpd.conf":
    source => "puppet:///apache/httpd.conf"
}

service { "httpd":
        enable      => "true",
        ensure      => "running",
        hasrestart => "true",
        hasstatus  => "true",
        require     => Package["httpd"]
}
}
```

Listing 4-19 defines the apache class that installs our required Apache packages, installs the httpd.conf configuration file, and then ensures the httpd service is started and running. You'll also notice we've specified the hasrestart and hasstatus attributes on the service. This tells Puppet that the init script for the service supports the restart and status commands. This lets Puppet know that the init script has more functionality and makes interacting with the script more flexible.

Next, in Listing 4-20, you'll find the apache::apache_files definition, which provides some shortcuts to manage our Apache-related files.

Listing 4-20. The apache::apache_files *Definition*

```
define appache::apache_files($owner = root, $group = root, $mode = 644, ↪
$source, $backup = false, $recurse = false, $ensure = file) {

    file { $name:
        mode    => $mode,
        owner   => $owner,
        group   => $group,
        backup  => $backup,
        recurse => $recurse,
        ensure  => $ensure,
        require => Package["httpd"],
        source  => "puppet:///httpd/$source"
    }
}
```

Lastly, in Listing 4-21 is the apache::virtual_host definition that allows us to create new virtual hosts on our web servers.

Listing 4-21. The apache::virtual_host *Definition*

```
define apache::virtual_host($ip, $ensure = "enabled") {
    $file = "/etc/httpd/conf.d/$name.conf"
    $document_root = "/var/www/html/$name"

    file { $file:
        ensure  => $ensure ? {
            enabled  => present,
            disabled => absent },
        content => template("apache/virtual_host.erb"),
        notify  => Service["httpd"]
    }
```

```
file { $document_root:
    ensure  => $ensure ? {
        enabled  => directory,
        disabled => absent },
    require => File["$file"]
}
}
```

The apache::virtual_host definition is included in the apache module and allows us to define one or more virtuals hosts. So how would we use this definition? Well, we'd invoke it in each node and for each virtual host we'd like to create. You can see this in Listing 4-22.

Listing 4-22. Using the apache::virtual_host *Definition*

```
node 'web.testing.com' inherits webserver {
   apache::virtual_host { "test1.testing.com":
       ip => "192.168.0.1"
   }
   apache::virtual_host { "test2.testing.com":
       ip => "192.168.0.2"
   }
}
```

Listing 4-22 shows the definition of the web.testing.com node. We invoke the apache::virtual_host definition twice. Each time the definition creates a configuration file in the /etc/httpd/conf.d/ directory that is based on the virtual_host.erb template. You can see this template here:

```
<VirtualHost <%= ip %>>
DocumentRoot <%= document_root %>
ServerName <%= name %>
</VirtualHost>
```

The template is populated with the document root, the IP address, and the server name variables from the definition. The resulting file for the first invokation of the apache::virtual_host definition would look like this:

```
<VirtualHost 192.168.0.1>
DocumentRoot /var/www/html/test1.testing.com
ServerName test1.testing.com
</VirtualHost>
```

Next, a directory is created for each virtual host to hold the site's files. Lastly, the definition triggers a reload of the httpd service with the use of the notify metaparameter.

If we wanted to remove a virtual host, we would set the ensure attribute to disabled in the definition like so:

```
virtual_host { "test1.testing.com":
    ip      => "192.168.0.1",
    ensure => disabled
}
```

This would remove the test1.testing.com configuration files and the associated directory. The httpd service would then be restarted to update Apache with the new configuration.

And again in Listing 4-4, you'll see that we have included the apache module in our templates.pp file as part of the webserver template node.

Resources

There are a lot of examples of Puppet configurations, especially modules. Listed here are some of these examples:

- *Reductive Labs Puppet module page, which includes modules for xen, git, and ntp, among others*:

  http://reductivelabs.com/trac/puppet/wiki/PuppetModules

- *Reductive Labs wiki page, which details module organization*:

  http://reductivelabs.com/trac/puppet/wiki/ModuleOrganisation

- *Puppet Show—a Ruby on Rails tool for managing Puppet including nodes and configuration*:

  http://reductivelabs.com/trac/puppet/wiki/PuppetShow

- *A CPAN-like way of distributing Puppet modules*:

  http://reductivelabs.com/trac/puppet/wiki/PuppetRecipeManager

- *A collection of Puppet recipes for configuring a variety of resources, applications, and daemons*:

  http://reductivelabs.com/trac/puppet/tags/puppet%2Crecipe

- *A Git repository containing a collection of modules*:

  `http://modules.reductivelabs.com/`

- *David Schmitt's collection of Puppet configuration and modules*:

  `http://git.black.co.at/?p=manifests.git;a=tree`

- *Modules for managing daemontools and djbdns*:

  `http://svn.dpiddy.net/projects/puppet/modules/`

- *Suggested template for documenting manifests*:

  `http://reductivelabs.com/trac/puppet/wiki/DocumentingManifests`

- *David Lutter's sample Puppet deployment*:

  `http://people.redhat.com/dlutter/puppet-app.html`

CHAPTER 5

Reporting on Puppet

One of the key aspects of any configuration management system is reporting. Reporting on a configuration management system can provide information on performance and compliance to policy and standards, and provide graphical representations of the overall state of your configuration. Puppet's reporting engine is limited at this stage but still allows some useful, albeit basic, reporting that can be graphed and displayed.

In this chapter, I'll explain what reports are available and how to work with them, look at graphing our reporting data, and briefly discuss how to build custom reports.

Getting Started

Puppet clients can be configured to return data at the end of each configuration run. Puppet calls this data a *transaction report*. The transaction reports are sent to the master server, where a number of report processors exist that can utilize this data and present it in a variety of forms. You can also develop your own report processors to customize the reporting output.

Each transaction report comes in the form of the YAML file. YAML, which is a recursive acronym for "YAML Ain't Markup Language," is a human-readable data serialization format that draws heavily from concepts in XML and the Python and C programming languages.

The transaction reports contain all log messages generated by the transaction and some additional metrics. The metrics fall into three general types: time, resource, and change metrics. Within each of these metrics are one or more values. They include the following:

- Transaction metric showing the time taken by the transaction
- Resource metrics including
    - *Total*: Total number of resources being managed
    - *Skipped*: Total resources that were skipped

- *Scheduled*: Total resources that were scheduled

- *Out of Sync*: Total resources that were out of sync

- *Applied*: Total resources that were applied

- *Failed*: Total resources that were not successfully applied

- *Restarted*: Total resources that were restarted through dependency changes

- *Failed Restarts*: Total resources that failed to be restarted after dependency changes

- Change metric showing the total number of changes that occurred in the transaction

In Listing 5-1, you can see an example of a Puppet transaction report.

Listing 5-1. Puppet Transaction Report

```
--- !ruby/object:Puppet::Transaction::Report
host: puppetmaster.testing.org
logs: []

metrics:
  time: !ruby/object:Puppet::Util::Metric
    label: Time
    name: time
    values:
    - - :service
      - Service
      - 0.189609050750732
    - - :total
      - Total
      - 3.7974648475647
    - - :config_retrieval
      - Config retrieval
      - 3.6055018901825
    - - :package
      - Package
      - 0.00235390663146973
  resources: !ruby/object:Puppet::Util::Metric
    label: Resources
    name: resources
```

```
    values:
    - - :failed_restarts
      - Failed restarts
      - 0
    - - :out_of_sync
      - Out of sync
      - 0
    - - :failed
      - Failed
      - 0
    - - :total
      - Total
      - 12
    - - :applied
      - Applied
      - 0
    - - :skipped
      - Skipped
      - 0
    - - :scheduled
      - Scheduled
      - 6
    - - :restarted
      - Restarted
      - 0
  changes: !ruby/object:Puppet::Util::Metric
    label: Changes
    name: changes
    values:
    - - :total
      - Total
      - 0
records: {}

time: 2007-09-18 10:59:12.567042 +10:00
```

In Listing 5-1, you can see the YAML file is divided into sections. The first section contains any log messages, and the following sections detail the value of each metric that Puppet collects. Each metric has a label, name, and values that make it easy to parse the data if you wish to make use of it for reporting or manipulation. The YAML format is very well supported by Ruby and can be easily utilized in Ruby to make use of Puppet reporting data.

Configuring Reporting

In order to get Puppet to output the reports we want, we need to configure it correctly. By default, each client is configured not to report back to the master, and reporting needs to be enabled. The first step to doing this is to ensure that the puppetd daemon on the client is started with the --report option like so:

```
# puppetd --report
```

This will cause the puppetd daemon to start creating and sending reports to the master. You could also set the report option in the puppet.conf configuration file:

```
[puppetd]
report = true
```

Tip ➡ By default, the client will send the reports back to the master configuring it. You can set up a separate Puppet master for reports only, if you like. You can then direct all reports to this server by using the reportserver option on the client. We'll discuss this in more detail in Chapter 6.

By default, the reports generated by the client will be sent to the master and stored as YAML-formatted files in the report directory. These files are the output of the default report processor, store. Reports are written into subdirectories under the report directory and a directory created for each client that is reporting. Report file names are the date stamp when the report was generated and are suffixed with .yaml, for example, 200710130604.yaml.

The report directory is $vardir/reports (usually /var/puppet/reports on most distributions), but you can override this by configuring the reportdir option on the master puppet.conf configuration file, like so:

```
[puppetmasterd]
reportdir = /etc/puppet/reports
```

Here we've set the new report directory to /etc/puppet/reports. You can specify whichever directory suits your environment.

Report Processors

There a number of different report processors available on the master server. The default report, store, simply stores the report file on the disk. There is also the log processor that sends logs to the local log destination, for example, to syslog. Also available is the tagmail report processor that sends e-mail messages based on particular tags in transaction reports. Lastly, the rrdgraph report processor converts transaction reports into RRD-based graphs.

Selecting which report processors will run is done using the reports configuration option in the puppet.conf configuration file.

```
[puppetmasterd]
reports = store,log,tagmail,rrdgraph
```

Each report processor you want to enable should be listed in the reports option with multiple processors separated by commas. By default, only store is enabled. You can also enable report processors on the command line.

```
# puppetmasterd --reports log,tagmail
```

log

The log report processor sends the log entries from transaction reports to syslog. It is the most simple of the report processors. The syslog destination facility is controlled by the syslogfacility configuration option, which defaults to the daemon facility.

```
[puppetmasterd]
syslogfacility = user
```

On the previous line, we've directed all syslog output to the user facility.

Note ➡ The log report processor only logs entries if the Puppet master is running in daemon mode. If you keep it running in the foreground, no syslog messages will be generated.

---

tagmail

The tagmail report sends log messages via e-mail based on the tags that are present in each log message. Remember, as we discussed in Chapter 3, tags allow you to set context for your resources; for example, you can tag all resources that belong to a particular operating system, location, or any other characteristic. Tags can also be specified in your puppet.conf configuration file to tell your clients to only apply configuration tagged with the specified tags.

The tagmail report uses these same tags to generate e-mail reports. The tags assigned to your resources are added to the log results, and then Puppet generates e-mails based on matching particular tags with particular e-mail addresses. The tags are matched with particular e-mail addresses in a configuration file called tagmail.conf. By default, the tagmail.conf file is located in $confdir directory, usually /etc/puppet. This is controlled by the tagmap configuration option in the puppet.conf file.

```
[puppetmasterd]
tagmap = $confdir/tagmail.conf
```

The tagmail.conf file contains a list of tags and e-mail addresses separated by colons. Multiple tags and e-mail addresses can be specified by separating them with commas. You can see an example of this file in Listing 5-2.

Listing 5-2. The tagmail.conf *Configuration File*

```
all:                    configuration@testing.org
melbourne, sydney:       aust_config@testing.org
dbserver, !oracle:      db_config@testing.org,mysql_config@testing.org
```

The first tag in Listing 5-2, all, is a special tag that tells Puppet to send all messages to the specified e-mail address.

Tip ➡ There is another special tag, called err. Specifying this tag will send all error messages generated during a configuration run to a particular e-mail address.

The next tags tell Puppet to send all log messages tagged with the tags melbourne and sydney to the e-mail address aust_config@testing.org. The last tags tell Puppet to send messages for all log entries with the dbserver tag but not the oracle tag to both the db_config@testing.org and mysql_config@testing.org e-mail addresses. You can see that the oracle tag has been negated using the ! symbol.

rrdgraph

One of the more useful built-in report processors is the rrdgraph type that takes advantage of Tobias Oetiker's RRD graphing libraries. The rrdgraph report processor generates RRD files, graphs, and some HTML files to display those graphs. It is a very quick and easy way to implement graphs of your Puppet configuration activities.

In order to make use of this report processor, we'll first need to install the RRDTools and the Ruby bindings for RRD. We can install RRDTools via package, and most platforms and distributions have a package for RRDTools. The Ruby bindings, unfortunately, are less well supported on a lot of platforms. They can be installed from source, or some distributions have packages available. There are also suitable rrdtool-ruby RPMs that should work on most RPM-based distributions like Red Hat, CentOS, and Mandriva versions available at Dag Wieer's repository at http://dag.wieers.com/rpm/packages/rrdtool/. There is also a development package for Gentoo called ruby-rrd that provides the required bindings that you should be able to install via emerge.

You can see a list of the required packages for various platforms in Table 5-1.

Table 5-1. Package Names for RRDTools

OS	Packages
Debian	rrdtool librrd2 librrd2-dev
FreeBSD	rrdtool
Fedora	rrdtool rrdtool-ruby
Gentoo	rrdtool ruby-rrd

(Continued)

OS	Packages
Mandriva	rrdtool
	rrdtool-ruby
NetBSD	rrdtool
OpenBSD	rrdtool
Red Hat	rrdtool
	rrdtool-ruby
SuSE	rrdtool
Ubuntu	rrdtool

Note ➡ Your package manager may also prompt you to install additional packages when installing RRDTool.

If there is not a Ruby bindings package for your platform, you can install the bindings via source. First, download the latest bindings package from RubyForge (at the time of writing, this was version 0.6.0), unpack it, and change into the resulting directory.

```
# wget http://rubyforge.org/frs/download.php/13992/RubyRRDtool-0.6.0.tgz
# tar -zxf RubyRRDtool-0.6.0.tgz
# cd RubyRRDtool-0.6.0
# ruby extconf.rb
# make
# make install
```

You will also need to configure three configuration options in the puppet.conf configuration file.

```
[puppetmasterd]
rrddir = $vardir/rrd
rrdinternval = $runinterval
rrdgraph = true
```

The rrddir directory specifies the default location for the generated RRD files; it defaults to $vardir/rrd, which is usually /var/puppet/rrd. The rrdinterval specifies how often RRD should expect to receive data. This defaults to $runinterval so as to match how often clients report back to the master. The last option, rrdgraph, turns on RRD graphing if set to true.

Turnbull

Underneath the $vardir/rrd directory, Puppet will create a directory for each node that reports to the master. Graphs (and associated HTML files to display them) will be generated in that directory. A graph will be generated for each metric that Puppet collects. You can then serve this directory out using your web server and display the graphs.

Custom Reporting

You are not limited to the provided report processors either. Puppet also allows you to create your own report processors. There are two methods for this. The first method is to use the existing store reports, which are YAML files, and write an external report processor to make use of this information, for example, graphing it or storing it in an external database. These external report processors are usually written in Ruby to take advantage of Ruby's ability to deserialize YAML files and make use of the resulting objects.

The second method involves writing your own report processor and adding it to Puppet. The report processors are stored in the lib/puppet/reports directory. On a Debian host, we'd add our custom report processor to the /usr/local/lib/site_ruby/1.8/puppet/reports directory with the existing report processors. We would then specify the new report in the reports configuration option.

The existing report processors make excellent templates for new processors. In Listing 5-3, you can see the Ruby code for the log report processor.

Listing 5-3. The log *Report Processor*

```
require 'puppet'
Puppet::Network::Handler.report.newreport(:log) do
    desc "Send all received logs to the local log destinations.  Usually
        the log destination is syslog."

    def process
        self.logs.each do |log|
            Puppet::Util::Log.newmessage(log)
        end
    end
end
```

It's very easy to create your own based on this template. First, you need to require Puppet by specifying require 'puppet'. Then you simply call the Puppet::Network::Handler.report.newreport function and specify the name of the new report processor you are creating, for example:

```
Puppet::Network::Handler.report.newreport(:mysql) do
```

Include a desc to describe the report processor and then specify the functionality of your report processor.

Resources

- *Details of available reports and reporting functionality*:

  http://reductivelabs.com/trac/puppet/wiki/ReportsAndReporting
- *Reference page detailing reports and their structure*:

  http://reductivelabs.com/trac/puppet/wiki/ReportReference

## CHAPTER 6

Advanced Puppet

In previous chapters, I have introduced you to Puppet and how to use it. In this chapter, we're going to look at some important advanced features available in Puppet. Specifically, we're going to look at three features: external nodes, LDAP nodes, and some methods for enhancing Puppet's scalability.

External nodes provide the capability to store our node definitions in a data source external to Puppet, for example, generated by a script or drawn from a database. An extension of this functionality, LDAP nodes, allows you to store your node configurations in a LDAP server. This externalization of data provides a number of advantages when managing our configuration information, especially in providing a single source of truth and a centralized repository for asset and configuration information.

As discussed in Chapter 1, the Puppet client-server model is not yet fully scalable to large installations, for example, the management of thousands of nodes. In this chapter, I'll examine using the Mongrel web server in combination with an Apache proxy running the `mod_ssl` and `mod_proxy_balancer` modules to enhance Puppet's scalability and allow you to run multiple master daemons.

External Node Classification

External nodes are node definitions stored externally to Puppet. To use external nodes, you need to construct a script that takes a hostname as an argument and returns information about that host. These scripts are known as *classifiers*. The information returned should be the classes that are to be included in the node and any variables we want to set.

Tip ➡ Puppet external nodes override node definitions in your manifest files. If you define external node classification, you must define all nodes in your node classifier.

To function correctly, the script must return the data in the form of a YAML hash, and the script must end with a zero exit code. A nonzero exit code will result in the configuration not being applied. The YAML hash can contain either classes or parameters or both.

To use external nodes, we first need to tell Puppet to use a classifier script to configure our nodes. To do this, we specify the script in the external_nodes configuration option in the [main] section of our puppet.conf file as you can see in Listing 6-1.

Listing 6-1. external_nodes *Configuration Option*

```
[main]
external_nodes = /usr/bin/puppet_node_classifier
```

In Listing 6-1, we've specified a classifier script called puppet_node_classifier located in the /usr/bin directory.

In the forthcoming 0.24 release of Puppet, you will also need to add an additional configuration option, node_terminus, to your puppet.conf configuration file.

```
[main]
node_terminus = exec
external_nodes = /usr/bin/puppet_node_classifier
```

The node_terminus configuration option is used to configure Puppet for node sources other than the default flat-file manifests. The exec option tells Puppet to use an external node classifier script.

Our classifier scripts can be written in any language, for example, shell script, Ruby, Perl, Python, or a variety of other languages. The only requirement is that the language must be able to output the appropriate YAML data. For example, you could also easily add a database back end to a classifier that queries a database for the relevant hostname and returns the associated classes and any variables.

In Listing 6-2, you can see a very simple node classifier written in shell script.

Listing 6-2. Simple Node Classifier

```
#!/bin/sh
cat <<"END"
---
classes:
  - baseapps
parameters:
  puppet_server: puppet.testing.com
END
exit 0
```

The script in Listing 6-2 will return the same classes and variables each time it is called regardless of what hostname is passed to the script.

```
$ puppet_node_classifier webserver.testing.com
---
classes:
  - baseapps
parameters:
  puppet_server: puppet.testing.com
```

Puppet will use this data to construct a node definition like that you can see in Listing 6-3.

Listing 6-3. Node Definition from Listing 6-2 Script

```
node webserver.testing.com {
        $puppet_server = 'puppet.testing.com'
        include baseapps
}
```

In Listing 6-3, `webserver.testing.com` would be replaced with the name of the host passed to the classifier as a variable.

More complex variations of this script could return different results depending on the particular hostname being passed to the classifier, in the same way different nodes would be configured with different classes, definitions, and variables in your manifest files. In Listing 6-4, you can see a more sophisticated node classifier written in Perl.

Listing 6-4. More Complex Perl-Based Node Classifier

```perl
#!/usr/bin/perl -w
use strict;
use YAML qw( Dump );

my $hostname = shift || die "No hostname passed";

$hostname =~ /^(\w+)\.(\w+)\.(\w{3})$/
    or die "Invalid hostname: $hostname";

my ( $host, $domain, $net ) = ( $1, $2, $3 );

my @classes = ( 'baseapps', $domain );
my %parameters = (
    puppet_server   => "puppet.$domain.$net"
    );
```

```
print Dump( {
    classes      => \@classes,
    parameters   => \%parameters,
} );
```

In Listing 6-4, we've created a Perl node classifier that makes use of the Perl YAML module. The YAML module can be installed via CPAN or your distribution's package management system. For example, on Debian it is the `libyaml-perl` package, or on Fedora it is the `perl-YAML` package. The classifier slices our hostname into sections; it assumes the input will be a fully qualified domain name and will fail if no hostname or an inappropriately structured hostname is passed. The classifier then uses those sections to classify the nodes and set parameters. If we called this node classifier with the hostname webserver.testing.com, it would return a node classification of

```
---
classes:
  - baseapps
  - testing
parameters:
  puppet_server: puppet.testing.com
```

This would result in a node definition in Puppet structured like

```
node 'webserver.testing.com' {
        include baseapps, testing

        $puppet_server = "puppet.testing.com"
}
```

Lastly, as discussed, we could also back-end our node classification script with a database as you can see in Listing 6-5.

Listing 6-5. A Database Back-End Node Classifier

```
#!/usr/bin/perl -w
use strict;
use YAML qw( Dump );
use DBI;

my $hostname = shift || die "No hostname passed";

$hostname =~ /^(\w+)\.(\w+)\.(\w{3})$/
    or die "Invalid hostname: $hostname";
```

Turnbull

```perl
my ( $host, $domain, $net ) = ( $1, $2, $3 );

# MySQL Configuration
my $data_source = "dbi:mysql:database=puppet;host=localhost";
my $username = "puppet";
my $password = "password";

# Connect to the server
my $dbh = DBI->connect($data_source, $username, $password)
    or die $DBI::errstr;

# Build the query
my $sth = $dbh->prepare( qq{SELECT class FROM nodes WHERE node = '$hostname'})
    or die "Can't prepare statement: $DBI::errstr";

# Execute the query
my $rc = $sth->execute
    or die "Can't execute statement: $DBI::errstr";

# Set parameters
my %parameters = (
    puppet_server   => "puppet.$domain.$net"
    );

# Set classes
my @class;
while (my @row=$sth->fetchrow_array)
 { push(@class,@row) }

# Check for problems
die $sth->errstr if $sth->err;

# Disconnect from database
$dbh->disconnect;

# Print the YAML
print Dump( {
    classes     => \@class,
    parameters  => \%parameters,
} );
```

The node classifier in Listing 6-5 would connect to a MySQL database called puppet running on the local host. Using the hostname, the script receiving it would query the database and return a list of classes to assign to the node. The nodes and classes would be stored in a table. The next lines comprise a SQL statement to create a very simple table to do this.

```
CREATE TABLE `nodes` (
`node` varchar(80) NOT NULL,
`class` varchar(80) NOT NULL ) TYPE=MyISAM;
```

The classes, and whatever parameters we set (which you could also place in the database in another table), are then returned and outputted as the required YAML data.

All of these external node classifiers are very simple and could easily be expanded upon to provide more sophisticated functionality. It is important to remember that external nodes override node configuration in your manifest files. If you enable an external node classifier, any node definitions in your manifest files will not be processed and will in fact be ignored by Puppet.

Note ➡ In Puppet versions earlier than 0.23, external node scripts were structured differently. I'm not going to cover these earlier scripts, but you can read about them at http://reductivelabs.com/trac/puppet/wiki/ExternalNodes.

Storing Node Configuration in LDAP

In addition to scripted external classification, Puppet also allows the storage of node information in an LDAP directory. This allows organizations to leverage already existing asset stores that are stored in LDAP directories or to decouple their configuration from Puppet and centralize it. Additionally, it also allows LDAP-enabled applications to have access to your configuration data.

Note ➡ Like external node classification, the use of LDAP nodes overrides node definitions in your manifest files. If you use LDAP node definitions, you cannot define nodes in your manifest files.

The first step in using LDAP for our node configuration is to ensure the Ruby LDAP libraries are installed. First, check for the presence of the LDAP libraries.

```
# ruby -rldap -e "puts :installed"
```

If this command does not return `installed`, the libraries are not installed. You can either install them via your distribution's package management system or download them from the Ruby/LDAP site. In Table 6-1, you can see a list of the currently available Ruby/LDAP packages for a variety of distributions.

Table 6-1. Package Names for Ruby LDAP Libraries

OS	Package
Debian	libldap-ruby1.8
FreeBSD	ruby-ldap
Gentoo	ruby-ldap
Mandriva	ruby-ldap
NetBSD	ruby-ldap
OpenBSD	ruby-ldap
SuSE	ruby-ldap

If there isn't a package for your distribution, you can download the required libraries either in the form of an RPM or a source package from the Ruby/LDAP site. The Ruby/LDAP site is located at `http://ruby-ldap.sourceforge.net/`.

If you need to compile the libraries yourself, download the current version, 0.9.7 at the time of writing, and unpack it.

```
$ wget http://optusnet.dl.sourceforge.net/sourceforge/ruby-ldap/ ➥
ruby-ldap-0.9.7.tar.gz
$ tar -zxf ruby-ldap-0.9.7.tar.gz
$ cd ruby-ldap-0.9.7
```

To compile Ruby/LDAP you will also need the Ruby development headers (usually provided by your distribution's ruby-devel package).

```
$ ruby extconf.rb
$ make
# make install
```

You can check for successful installation with the `ruby -rldap -e "puts :installed"` command.

Next you need to set up your LDAP server. You can use OpenLDAP, Red Hat Directory Server (or Fedora Directory Server), Sun's Directory Server, or one of a variety of other LDAP servers. We're going to assume we are using OpenLDAP, and we're also going to assume we've already got it set up and running.

Tip ➡ For some quick start instructions on setting up OpenLDAP, you can refer to
`http://www.openldap.org/doc/admin23/quickstart.html`.

The first step we need to take for our LDAP configuration is to add the Puppet schema to our LDAP directory's configuration.

Caution ➡ You may need to tweak or translate the default LDAP schema for some directory servers, but it is suitable for OpenLDAP.

The Puppet schema document is available in the Puppet source package in the `ext/ldap/puppet.schema` file or can be taken from the project's Git repository at `http://reductivelabs.com/git/puppet/`. We need to add it to our schema directory and `slapd.conf` configuration file. For example, on a Debian host, the schema directory is `/etc/ldap/schema`, and the `slapd.conf` configuration is located in the `/etc/ldap` directory. Copy the `puppet.schema` file into the appropriate directory.

```
$ cp puppet-0.23.2/ext/ldap/puppet.schema /etc/ldap/schema/
```

Now we add an `include` statement to our `slapd.conf` configuration file; there should be a number of existing statements you can model.

```
include          /etc/ldap/schema/puppet.schema
```

To update OpenLDAP, we now need to restart our server.

```
# /etc/init.d/slapd restart
```

Once we've configured the LDAP server, we need to tell Puppet to use an LDAP server as the source of its node configuration. We configure this in the [puppetmasterd] section of the `puppet.conf` configuration file as you can see in Listing 6-6.

Listing 6-5. Puppet LDAP Configuration

```
[puppetmasterd]
ldapnodes = true
ldapserver = ldapserver.testing.com
ldapbase = ou=Hosts,dc=testing,dc=com
```

LDAP configuration is very simple. First, we set the ldapnodes option to true. Next we specify the hostname of our LDAP server, in our case ldapserver.testing.com, in the ldapserver option. Lastly, in the ldapbase option, we specify the base search path. Puppet recommends that hosts be stored in an OU called Hosts under our main directory structure, but you can configure this to suit your environment.

As with external nodes, in the forthcoming 0.24 release of Puppet you will also need to add the configuration option node_terminus to your puppet.conf configuration file. The ldapnodes configuration option will then become deprecated and should be removed.

```
[main]
node_terminus = ldap
```

As discussed previously the node_terminus configuration option is used to configure Puppet for node sources other than the default flat-file manifests. Here, using the ldap option tells Puppet to seek node configurations in an LDAP directory. All other configuration options remain the same.

If required, you can specify a user and password using the ldapuser and ldappassword options and override the default LDAP port of 389 with the ldapport option. There is some limited support for TLS or SSL, but only if your LDAP server does not require client-side certificates. You can see a full list of the potential LDAP options at http://reductivelabs.com/trac/puppet/wiki/ConfigurationReference.

After configuring Puppet to use LDAP nodes, you should restart your Puppet master daemon to ensure the new configuration is updated.

Now we need to add our node configuration to the LDAP server. Let's take a quick look at the Puppet LDAP schema in Listing 6-7.

Listing 6-7. The LDAP Schema

```
# These OIDs are all fake. No guarantees there won't be conflicts.
#
# $Id: puppet.schema 1260 2006-06-13 18:09:07Z luke $

attributetype ( 1.1.3.10 NAME 'puppetclass'
        DESC 'Puppet Node Class'
        EQUALITY caseIgnoreIA5Match
        SYNTAX 1.3.6.1.4.1.1466.115.121.1.26 )
```

```
attributetype ( 1.1.3.9 NAME 'parentnode'
       DESC 'Puppet Parent Node'
       EQUALITY caseIgnoreIA5Match
       SYNTAX 1.3.6.1.4.1.1466.115.121.1.26 )

objectclass ( 1.1.1.2 NAME 'puppetClient' SUP top AUXILIARY
       DESC 'Puppet Client objectclass'
       MAY ( puppetclass $ parentnode ))
```

Caution ➡ As the schema in Listing 6-7 indicates, the OIDs have been invented by Reductive. They could potentially conflict with other OIDs.

The Puppet schema is made up of an object class, puppetClient, and two attributes, puppetclass and parentnode. The object class puppetClient is assigned to each host that is a Puppet node. The puppetclass attribute contains all of the classes defined for that node. At this stage, you cannot add definitions, just classes. The parentnode attribute allows you to specify node inheritance.

In addition, any attributes defined in your LDAP node entries are available as variables to Puppet. This works much like Facter facts; for example, if the host entry has the ipHost class, the ipHostNumber attribute of the class is available as the variable $ipHostNumber. Attributes with multiple values are created as arrays.

You can also define default nodes in the same manner you can in your manifest node definitions, by creating a host in your directory called default. The classes assigned to this host will be applied to any node that does not match a node in the directory. If no default node exists and no matching node definition is found, Puppet will return an error.

You can now add your hosts, or the relevant object class and attributes to existing definitions for your hosts, in the LDAP directory. You can import your host definitions using LDIF files or manipulate your directory using your choice of tools such as phpldapadmin. In Listing 6-8 is an LDIF file containing examples of node definitions.

Listing 6-8. LDIF Nodes

```
# LDIF Export for: ou=Hosts,dc=testing,dc=com
dn: ou=Hosts,dc=testing,dc=com
objectClass: organizationalUnit
objectClass: top
ou: Hosts
```

```
dn: cn=default,ou=Hosts,dc=testing,dc=com
cn: default
description: Default
objectClass: device
objectClass: top
objectClass: puppetClient
puppetclass: defaultapps

dn: cn=basenode,ou=Hosts,dc=testing,dc=com
cn: basenode
description: Basenode
objectClass: device
objectClass: top
objectClass: puppetClient
puppetclass: baseapps

dn: cn=webserver,ou=Hosts,dc=testing,dc=com
cn: webserver
description: Webserver
objectClass: device
objectClass: top
objectClass: puppetClient
parentnode: basenode
puppetclass: apache
puppetclass: squid
puppetclass: named

dn: cn=www1.testing.com, ou=Hosts,dc=testing,dc=com
cn: www1
description: webserving host
objectclass: device
objectclass: top
objectclass: puppetClient
objectclass: ipHost
parentnode: webserver
ipHostNumber: 192.168.0.100
```

Listing 6-8 includes a default node, a node called basenode, and a template node called webserver. Each node has particular classes assigned to it, and the webserver node has the basenode defined as its parent node and thus inherits its classes also. Lastly, we define a client node, called www1, which inherits the webserver node as a parent.

Tip ➡ Also available to help manage nodes is the iClassify tool, which you can learn about at
`http://oss.hjksolutions.com/iclassify/`. You can download the code using Git from git clone
`git://hjksolutions.com/iclassify`.

Puppet Scalability

As discussed in Chapter 1, Puppet is not yet a fully scalable solution as it has no built-in
capability for high availability or load balancing between multiple masters. Additionally,
Puppet is not yet fully ready for an enterprise-wide deployment as the built-in WEBrick
web server, used to service the REST connections from Puppet clients, cannot yet scale to
large numbers of clients. When connected, large numbers of clients, especially those using
file serving, can cause performance issues and connection failures.

There are some workarounds for both high availability and load balancing. Solutions
like Heartbeat (`http://www.linux-ha.org/`), VRRP, or hardware load balancers can allow
multiple master servers to be represented by a single IP address. Configuration can be
shared between multiple masters using a distributed version control system like SVK (a
distributed enhancement to Subversion) or Git.

Another workaround uses the Mongrel web server in lieu of the built-in WEBrick web
server with a web proxy load balancing the client connections. This approach was
developed by Puppet author Luke Kanies, Debian developer Marcin Owsiany, and Jeff
McCune of the Ohio State University. In this section, I'm going to explain how to make use
of this method to allow your Puppet environment to service a larger number of clients.

Note ➡ Version 0.23.1 or later of Puppet is required to support this approach. Puppet masters and clients
using earlier versions do not correctly sign certificates.

The Puppet master daemon, `puppetmasterd`, normally uses the WEBrick web server
internally to connect clients, but Puppet also supports using Mongrel as an alternative web
server. Mongrel is commonly used as a web server by Ruby on Rails applications, and you
can learn more about it at `http://mongrel.rubyforge.org/`.

With Mongrel integrated with Puppet, multiple `puppetmasterd` daemons can be run, each
on a different port. A web server, in our case Apache, is placed in front of these instances,
and the `mod_proxy` and `mod_proxy_balancer` modules are used to load balance connections to
these instances.

Tip ➡ Rather than Apache, you could also use other web servers. Other good choices include servers like lighthttd or nginx or a load balancer such as Pound. You can find instructions for running Mongrel with Pound at `http://reductivelabs.com/trac/puppet/wiki/UsingMongrelPound` and with nginx at `http://reductivelabs.com/trac/puppet/wiki/UsingMongrelNginx`.

You can see a diagram that shows this architecture in Figure 6-1.

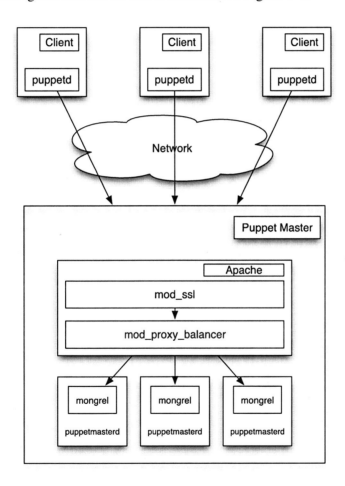

Figure 6-1. Puppet with Mongrel architecture

Installing Mongrel

The first step is to install Mongrel. There are three ways to install Mongrel—via package, via a Ruby Gem, or via source. In Table 6-2, I've listed the operating systems that currently have a package available for Mongrel. Also listed in Table 6-2 is the name of the relevant package. Your package management system may also prompt you to install additional packages.

Table 6-2. Mongrel Packages

OS	Package
FreeBSD	rubygem-mongrel
Gentoo	mongrel
NetBSD	mongrel
OpenBSD	ruby-mongrel
SuSE	rubygem-mongrel

You can also install Mongrel via a Ruby Gem if you have Ruby Gems installed.

```
# gem install mongrel
```

Like packages, gem may prompt you to install additional packages.

Lastly, you can download and install Mongrel from source like so:

```
# wget http://rubyforge.org/frs/download.php/27286/mongrel-1.1.tgz
# tar -zxf mongrel-1.1.tgz
# cd mongrel-1.1
# ruby setup.rb
```

We don't have to do anything to configure Mongrel. Puppet will do this for us when we start the Puppet daemon.

Installing Apache

Next we need to install Apache. Many hosts already have Apache installed, and the mod_proxy and mod_proxy_balancer modules we need are installed with it. But if you need to install Apache, you can do it via package or source. These packages generally also include all of the required modules we need to integrate Apache with Mongrel and Puppet, and you can see the list in Table 6-3.

Table 6-3. Apache Packages

OS	Package
Debian	apache2
Fedora	httpd
FreeBSD	apache2
Gentoo	apache
NetBSD	apache2
OpenBSD	apache-httpd
Red Hat	httpd
SuSE	apache2
Ubuntu	apache2

Your package management system may also prompt you to install additional packages as dependencies to Apache.

If you haven't got a suitable package, you can also download and install the latest version of Apache via source. I have chosen to download from a mirror in Australia, but you can check the Apache download page at http://httpd.apache.org/download.cgi to find an appropriate mirror. In Listing 6-9, we've downloaded, unpacked, and configured Apache.

Listing 6-9. Installing Apache from Source

```
$ wget http://apache.planetmirror.com.au/dist/httpd/httpd-2.2.6.tar.gz
$ tar -zxf httpd-2.2.6.tar.gz
$ cd httpd-2.2.6
$ configure --prefix=/usr/local/apache2 --enable-so --enable-proxy=shared ➥
--enable-proxy-balancer=shared --enable-authz_host=shared --enable-ssl=shared ➥
--enable-headers=shared --enable-proxy-http=shared
$ make
# make install
```

In Listing 6-9, we've configured (including enabled Apache modules), compiled, and installed Apache into the directory /usr/local/apache2.

Configuring Apache As a Proxy

After you've installed Apache, you need to configure it. To do this we need to configure a virtual host, proxy balancing, and SSL, which entails creating an SSL-enabled virtual host that will be proxy balanced back to our puppetmasterd daemons running Mongrel. You can see an example of a simple Apache configuration to do this in Listing 6-10.

Listing 6-10. Apache with Mongrel Configuration

```
Listen 8140
PidFile /var/www/puppet/run/balancer.pid
User puppet
Group puppet

LoadModule proxy_module modules/mod_proxy.so
LoadModule proxy_http_module modules/mod_proxy_http.so
LoadModule proxy_balancer_module modules/mod_proxy_balancer.so
LoadModule headers_module modules/mod_headers.so
LoadModule ssl_module modules/mod_ssl.so
LoadModule authz_host_module modules/mod_authz_host.so
LoadModule log_config_module modules/mod_log_config.so

<Directory />
    Options FollowSymLinks
    AllowOverride None
    Order deny,allow
    Deny from all
```

```
</Directory>

<Proxy balancer://puppetmaster.testing.com>
   BalancerMember http://127.0.0.1:18140 keepalive=on max=2 retry=30

   BalancerMember http://127.0.0.1:18141 keepalive=on max=2 retry=30

</Proxy>

<VirtualHost *:8140>
    SSLEngine on
    SSLCipherSuite SSLv2:-LOW:-EXPORT:RC4+RSA
    SSLCertificateFile     /var/www/puppet/ssl/certs/puppetmaster.testing.com.pem
    SSLCertificateKeyFile  /var/www/puppet/ssl/private_keys/ ➡
puppetmaster.testing.com.pem
    SSLCertificateChainFile /var/www/puppet/ssl/ca/ca_crt.pem
    SSLCACertificateFile    /var/www/puppet/ssl/ca/ca_crt.pem
    SSLCARevocationFile     /var/www/puppet/ssl/ca/ca_crl.pem
    SSLVerifyClient optional
    SSLVerifyDepth  1
    SSLOptions +StdEnvVars

    RequestHeader set X-SSL-Subject %{SSL_CLIENT_S_DN}e
    # Store the client DN in a header
    RequestHeader set X-Client-DN %{SSL_CLIENT_S_DN}e
    # And store whether the cert verification was a success
    RequestHeader set X-Client-Verify %{SSL_CLIENT_VERIFY}e

<Location />
       SetHandler balancer-manager
       Order allow,deny
       Allow from all
    </Location>

    ProxyPass / balancer://puppetmaster.testing.com:8140/ timeout=180
    ProxyPassReverse / balancer://puppetmaster.testing.com:8140/
    ProxyPreserveHost on
    SetEnv force-proxy-request-1.0 1
    SetEnv proxy-nokeepalive 1
```

```
ErrorLog   /var/www/puppet/balancer_error.log
    CustomLog /var/www/puppet/balancer_access.log combined
    CustomLog /var/www/puppet/balancer_ssl_request.log \
                "%t %h %{SSL_PROTOCOL}x %{SSL_CIPHER}x \"%r\" %b"
</VirtualHost>
```

Let's examine the configuration we've specified in Listing 6-10. We start by running Apache on port 8140 so that our clients don't require any reconfiguration to connect to our new proxy. Next, we specify a process ID file in a directory we're going to create for our server.

```
# mkdir -p /var/www/puppet/run
```

We then specify the user and group name that we want Apache to run as. This should be the same as the user and group that the `puppetmasterd` daemon runs as. In our case, this is the user and group `puppet`.

Then in Listing 6-10, we've specified a number of `LoadModule` statements. These load the required modules, such as the `mod_proxy_balancer` module, needed to run our Apache proxy. The required modules are as follows:

- `mod_proxy`

- `mod_proxy_http`

- `mod_proxy_balancer`

- `mod_headers`

- `mod_ssl`

- `mod_authz_host`

- `mod_log_config`

For Red Hat–style distributions, the Apache daemon tries to load all available modules, and you can see the `LoadModule` statements in your Apache configuration file, for example, /etc/httpd/conf/httpd.conf on a Red Hat platform, for the required modules. The `LoadModule` statements in Listing 6-10 assume our modules are in a directory called `modules` in the same directory as our configuration file is located.

```
LoadModule proxy_module modules/mod_proxy.so
```

For Debian-style distributions, including Ubuntu, you can use the `a2enmod` command to enable modules. Some modules may already be enabled. You can see the `a2enmod` command in Listing 6-11.

Listing 6-11. The a2enmod *Command*

```
a2enmod headers authz_host proxy proxy_balancer proxy_http ssl log_config
```

After our modules, we define a `Directory` block for the root of our proxy and then a `Proxy` block. Inside the `Proxy` block, we specify the hostname of our proxy, in our case `puppetmaster.testing.com`. We also specify each load balanced member of the proxy.

```
BalancerMember http://127.0.0.1:18140 keepalive=on max=2 retry=30
BalancerMember http://127.0.0.1:18141 keepalive=on max=2 retry=30
```

Each of these members represents a `puppetmasterd` instance running Mongrel. In our configuration, each instance is started on a separate port on the local host, in our case ports 18140 and 18141. We can add as many instances as required. It is good practice to create instances by incrementing the port number, and we'll see how to do this later when we configure the Puppet master to support this configuration.

Then we configure our virtual host, again ensuring we specify the 8140 port. We turn on SSL for the virtual host and configure the location of our certificate files. These certificates are the Puppet certificates our master currently uses. The easiest way to do this is to create a symbolic link from the Puppet SSL directory, usually `/etc/puppet/ssl`, to our proxy directory, in our case `/var/www/puppet`.

```
# ln -s /etc/puppet/ssl /var/www/puppet/ssl
```

We then specify our Puppet master's certificate and key file, and then the associated Certificate Authority (CA) certificate and certificate revocation list. Also inside our virtual host definition we define our `ProxyPass` statement that enables the proxy; you would replace `puppetmaster.testing.com` with the hostname of your proxy server.

Lastly, we specify the location, in our case `/var/www/puppet`, of a variety of logging files.

After configuring Apache, we need to start our Apache daemon. You can do this by running the Apache binary, for example, `httpd` on Red Hat–style hosts and `apache2` on Debian-style hosts, and specifying the name of our configuration file.

```
# httpd -f /etc/httpd/puppet.conf
```

Or

```
# apache2 -f /etc/apache2/puppet.conf
```

You could also integrate your Puppet proxy configuration into your existing Puppet configuration. Many distributions have a `conf.d` directory, for example, on Red Hat it's `/etc/httpd/conf.d/`, in which you can locate configuration files. You would then restart your Apache daemon to enable the new configuration.

Configuring Puppet for Mongrel

Enabling the Mongrel integration for Puppet is very simple. We start the puppetmasterd daemon with the --servertype mongrel option. To specify multiple puppetmasterd instances, we start each puppetmasterd with a different master port and process ID file.

```
# puppetmasterd --servertype mongrel --masterport 18140 ➡
--pid /var/www/puppet/run/puppetmasterd.18140.pid
```

We would then start the next instance with our port number incremented like so:

```
# puppetmasterd --servertype mongrel --masterport 18141 ➡
--pid /var/www/puppet/run/puppetmasterd.18141.pid
```

In Listing 6-12, you can see a simple script that you could easily convert into an init script, which allows you to start multiple puppetmasterd instances.

Listing 6-12. Puppet Master with Mongrel Initiation Script

```
#!/bin/bash
# name: mongrel_puppetmasterd
# Start a Puppet Master Server instance.

if ! [[ "$1" -gt 0 ]]; then
echo "ERROR: You must provide a port to run this puppet master on."
echo "Ensure your apache load balancer is configured to talk to these servers"
exit 1
fi

MASTERPORT="$1"
shift

puppetmasterd \
--pidfile=/var/www/puppet/run/puppetmasterd."${MASTERPORT}".pid \
--servertype=mongrel \
--masterport="${MASTERPORT}" \
$*
```

We would run the script in Listing 6-12 and pass in a variable for our master port like so:

```
# mongrel_puppetmasterd 18140
```

We can now start as many Mongrel Puppet master instances as we like and our master host can sustain.

How Far Will Puppet Scale?

At this stage of Puppet development, there are no clear performance statistics regarding either the WEBrick or Mongrel web servers. Anecdotal evidence and some limited testing (conducted by Jeff McCune) indicate that the Mongrel web server is approximately 50% faster than the WEBrick web server. You can see the results of this indicative testing at `http://reductivelabs.com/trac/puppet/wiki/PuppetScalability#MasterCompileTimings`. The enhanced performance should extend Puppet's ability to service nodes and allow the connection of potentially thousands of nodes. At this stage, insufficient testing has been performed to determine exactly how many nodes can be connected and what volume of file serving and configuration supported for each node. The replacement of the XML-RPC architecture with a REST-based architecture is also likely to improve the performance of both the WEBrick and Mongrel web servers.

Resources

The following links will take you to Puppet documentation related to external nodes and Puppet scalability:

* *Using external nodes in Puppet*:

    `http://reductivelabs.com/trac/puppet/wiki/ExternalNodes`
* *LDAP nodes in Puppet*:

    `http://reductivelabs.com/trac/puppet/wiki/LdapNodes`
* *Using Mongrel with Puppet*:

    `http://reductivelabs.com/trac/puppet/wiki/UsingMongrel`
* *Using Mongrel with Pound*:

    `http://reductivelabs.com/trac/puppet/wiki/UsingMongrelPound`
* *Using Mongrel with nginx*:

    `http://reductivelabs.com/trac/puppet/wiki/UsingMongrelNginx`

- *Puppet scalability documentation*:

  http://reductivelabs.com/trac/puppet/wiki/PuppetScalability

## CHAPTER 7

Extending Puppet

Among the most powerful features of both Puppet and Facter are their flexibility and extensibility. In addition to the existing resource types and facts, you can quickly and easily add custom types and facts specific to your environment or to meet a particular need. In this chapter, we're going to examine how to add your own custom facts to Facter, have Puppet automatically distribute those facts, and then see how to make use of them. I'm also going to demonstrate how to create a simple resource type (and associated provider) for Puppet and how to integrate that new resource type into your Puppet installation. This chapter, however, is just an introduction to extending Puppet. If you want to learn more, there is extensive documentation available on the Puppet Wiki and on the Puppet Developer mailing list.

When developing custom types and facts, it is important to remember that Puppet and Facter are open source tools developed both by Reductive Labs and a wide community of contributors. Sharing custom facts and resource types helps everyone in the community and means you can also get input from the community on your work. Extending Puppet or Facter is also an excellent way to give back to that community. You can share your custom types and facts via the Puppet mailing list, on the Puppet Wiki, logging a Trac ticket, or setting up your own source repository for Puppet or Facter code.

Tip ➡ We aren't going to discuss it in this chapter, but you can also extend Puppet by creating your own functions. You can see more details of this at
`http://reductivelabs.com/trac/puppet/wiki/WritingYourOwnFunctions`.

Extending Facter

Adding your own custom facts to Puppet is a very simple process that requires only a limited understanding of Ruby. To add a new fact, we add a snippet of Ruby code to our Puppet master. Puppet then distributes our custom facts to all our clients using a function called factsync. Each client that connects to the master gets all the facts available synchronized down to it.

Configuring Puppet for Custom Facts

We start with telling Puppet to turn on fact synchronization using the factsync configuration option. We then specify where Puppet will find our facts using the factpath configuration option. You can see both these options in Listing 7-1.

Listing 7-1. Fact Synchronization

```
[puppetmasterd]
factsync = true
factpath = $vardir/facts
```

In Listing 7-1, we've turned on fact synchronize and specified the path, in our case $vardir/facts, which on most installations would default to /var/puppet/facts, where our facts will be located on our master. You can specify multiple paths by separating each with colons.

By default, with factsync enabled, Puppet clients look for facts at puppet://$server/facts much like file serving.

Tip ➡ Remember, $server is a fact with the hostname of our Puppet master that is only available on the master.

Each fact is treated as a file resource and served out by the built-in Puppet file server. As factsync uses the built-in file server, you can use any valid file source to deliver your facts. To override the default file source for facts, use the factsource configuration option.

Tip ➡ File serving is described in Chapter 4.

Facts are downloaded to our clients and stored in a local directory, usually also $vardir/facts on the client, but this can be overridden using the factdest configuration option (though obviously only one destination path can be configured).

After restarting the master daemon, Puppet will now be ready to deliver facts to your client nodes. These facts are then available to your configuration as variables in the same way as the facts provided by Facter.

Tip ➡ There are other configuration options you can use to tweak your fact configuration that you can read about at `http://reductivelabs.com/trac/puppet/wiki/ConfigurationReference`.

Writing Custom Facts

After configuring Puppet to deliver our custom facts, we actually need to create some new facts. As we mentioned, our custom facts are snippets of Ruby code that call the `Facter.add` function to add new facts. In Listing 7-2, you can see a simple custom fact.

Listing 7-2. Our First Custom Fact

```
Facter.add("home") do
      setcode do
           ENV['HOME']
      end
end
```

In Listing 7-2, our custom fact returns the value of the `HOME` environmental value as a fact called `home`, which in turn would be available in our manifests as the variable `$home`.

Let's break down Listing 7-2. The `Facter.add` function allows us to specify the name of our new fact. We then use the `setcode` block to specify the contents of our new fact, in our case using Ruby's built-in `ENV` variable to access an environmental variable. In Listing 7-3, we can see a custom fact that reads a file to return the value of the fact.

Listing 7-3. Another Custom Fact

```
Facter.add("timezone") do
      confine :operatingsystem => :debian
      setcode do
           File.readlines("/etc/timezone").to_a.last
      end
end
```

In Listing 7-3, we're returning the timezone of a Debian host. In Listing 7-3, we've also done two interesting things. First, we've specified a `confine` statement. This statement restricts the execution of the fact if a particular criteria is not met. This restriction is commonly implemented by taking advantage of the values of other facts. In this case, we've specified that the value of the `operatingsystem` fact should be Debian for the fact to be executed. We can also use the values of other facts, for example:

```
confine :kernel => :linux
```

The previous `confine` is commonly used to limit the use of a particular fact to nodes with Linux-based kernels.

Second, we've used the `readlines` file method to read in the contents of the /etc/timezone file. The contents are returned as the fact `timezone`, which in turn would be available as the variable `$timezone`.

```
timezone => Australia/Melbourne
```

You can create more complex facts and even return more than one fact in your Ruby snippets as you can see in Listing 7-4.

Listing 7-4. A More Complex Fact

```
        netname = nil
        netaddr = nil
        test = {}
        File.open("/etc/networks").each do |line|
            netname = $1 and netaddr = $2 if line ➥
=~ /^(\w+.?\w+)\s+([0-9]+\.[0-9]+\.[0-9]+\.[0-9]+)/
            if netname != nil && netaddr != nil
                test["network_" + netname] = netaddr
                netname = nil
                netaddr = nil
            end
    end
       test.each{|name,fact|
                Facter.add(name) do
                    confine :operatingsystem => :debian
                    setcode do
                        fact
                    end
                end
    }
```

In Listing 7-4, you can see a more complicated fact. This fact actually creates a series of facts, each fact taken from information collected from the `/etc/networks` file. This file, used on Debian hosts, associates network names with networks. Our snippet parses this file and adds a series of facts, one per each network in the file. So that if our file looked like

```
default    0.0.0.0
loopback    127.0.0.0
link-local    169.254.0.0
```

then three facts would be returned:

```
default => 0.0.0.0
loopback => 127.0.0.0
link-local => 169.254.0.0
```

You can take a similar approach to commands, or files, or a variety of other sources.

Testing Your Facts

There is a simple process for testing your facts. We import our facts into Facter and use it to test them before making use of them in Puppet. To do this, we need to set up a testing environment. We create a directory structure to hold our test facts—we'll call ours `lib/ruby/facter`. We'll situate this structure beneath the `root` user's home directory. We then create an environmental variable, `$RUBYLIB`, that references this directory and will allow Facter to find our test facts.

```
# mkdir -p ~/lib/ruby/facter
# export RUBYLIB=~/lib/ruby
```

We then copy our fact snippets into this new directory.

```
# cp /var/puppet/facts/home.rb $RUBYLIB/facter
```

After this we can call Facter with the name of the fact we've just created. If the required output appears, your fact is working correctly. If your fact is not working correctly, an error message you can debug will be generated.

```
# facter home
/root
```

On the previous lines, we've tested our home fact and discovered it has returned the correct value.

Extending Puppet

When configuring your nodes, you are not limited to the resource types provided with Puppet. You can build your own resource types to manage additional configuration components and items. Custom resource types are developed in Ruby and like custom facts can be propagated by Puppet from your master to all of your clients.

Tip ➡ Your best source of information about how to build your own types and providers are the existing types and providers that come with Puppet. Among them you can find examples of most types of configuration management. I recommend reviewing them before embarking on creating a particular type or provider.

Each resource type should consist of the type definition and any required providers. The type creates the model for what the type actually does. It specifies the attributes and features available to configure your component, sets the valid parameters, and handles input validation. The provider or providers implement the type on a variety of platforms; for example, you might have a provider to implement your type on Linux platforms and another provider to provide the same functionality on a Solaris host. The provider performs the actions and implements the features defined in the type.

Tip ➡ Not all types need providers. Some simple types include all required functionality in the type definition. An example of this is the exec type.

I'm going to demonstrate how to build a very simple resource type. The type will manage the /etc/shells file. The /etc/shells file contains a list of the valid login shells on your host. Applications use this file to determine what shells are valid. Each shell is listed on a separate line and consists of the name of the shell and its path relative to the root directory, /. You can see an example of an /etc/shells file in Listing 7-5.

Listing 7-5. The /etc/shells *File*

```
/bin/sh
/bin/bash
/sbin/nologin
/bin/tcsh
/bin/csh
/bin/zsh
/bin/ksh
```

Tip ➡ Puppet best practice for type development has evolved and changed over Puppet's life. It will almost certainly continue to evolve. This section demonstrates current best practice.

Creating the Type

To manage our /etc/shells file, we first need to create a resource type definition. In Listing 7-6, you can see the skeleton of our shells type.

Listing 7-6. The shells.rb *Type Skeleton*

```
module Puppet
        newtype(:shells) do
        @doc = "Manages shells in /etc/shells. For example::

        shells { \"/bin/bash\":
            ensure => present,
        }

        There is also an optional target attribute if your
        shells file is located elsewhere."

        end
end
```

In Listing 7-6, we load the Puppet module and specify a new resource type, in our case shells. You should store your resource type in a file named for your type, in this case shells.rb.

Tip ➡ In the default Puppet installation, our resource types are located in the puppet/lib/type directory; for example, if we've installed from source on most Linux distributions, you'd find them at /usr/local/lib/site_ruby/1.8/puppet/lib/type.

We use @doc to document our type. In @doc, the documentation should be created in the form of reStructuredText (http://docutils.sourceforge.net/rst.html). It is always a good idea to include, as we have in Listing 7-6, examples of how the resource type should be used.

After creating our skeleton and documenting our type, we need to add the required attributes and features. You can see our complete shells type in Listing 7-7.

Listing 7-7. The Complete shells.rb *Type*

```
module Puppet
      newtype(:shells) do

      @doc = "Manages shells in /etc/shells. For example::

      shells { \"/bin/bash\":
         ensure => present,
      }
      There is also an optional target attribute if your
      shells file is located elsewhere."

      ensurable

      newparam(:shell, :namevar => true) do
         desc "The shell to manage"
         isnamevar
      end

      newproperty(:target) do
         desc "Location of shells file"
         defaultto { if @resource.class.defaultprovider.ancestors.include? ➡
(Puppet::Provider::ParsedFile)
                           @resource.class.defaultprovider.default_target
                     else
                           nil
                     end
         }
```

```
        end
     end
end
```

Resource types are principally made up of properties and parameters. In Listing 7-7, you can see a property and a parameter being defined and a method called ensurable being called.

Properties

Properties are the configurable elements of the resource type; for example, in the file resource type, the owner and mode attributes are both properties. They tell Puppet how to configure the resource being managed. Properties can have defaults set, contain input validation to ensure only specific values can be set, or perform munging on the value or values being set. Properties are defined using the newproperty method.

Properties interact with your providers, and the values they contain are used by providers to configure your resource on the target node. In our example of the file resource type, the value of the owner property is used to define the owner of the object being managed. The file resource provider then uses this value to set the owner of the object on the target node.

In Listing 7-7, we've only defined one property, target. This property tells Puppet the location of the /etc/shells file. It's optional and probably will be infrequently used, as almost all systems use the standard /etc/shells location for the shells file. For the value of this property, we've set a default. This default uses a helper class called ParsedFile that is used to parse files, and we'll look at that when we look at creating our provider.

While it is not explicitly a property, calling the ensurable helper method provides the functionality of the ensure property and adds the values present and absent to that property. The ensure property is frequently used in resource types as it creates and destroys resources. You will probably recognize it in the form of the ensure attribute.

```
ensure => present
ensure => absent
```

Parameters

Parameters are type definition variables that define how the resource will behave. An example of a parameter is the recurse attribute of the file resource type. If specified, this tells the resource whether to recurse through directories or not. In Listing 7-7, we've defined a parameter using the newparam method called shell, which is used to configure the exact shell we wish to install into the /etc/shells file.

In Listing 7-7, you can also see that we've added something to our shell parameter, isnamevar, that tells Puppet that this parameter is the attribute that sets the title or name of our type. Each type needs to have a parameter that is the name variable. In the Type Reference Wiki page (http://reductivelabs.com/trac/puppet/wiki/TypeReference), you can see that each type has a name variable defined.

Tip ➡ Both properties and parameters can have the desc method. This is used to document each property or parameter. You should always use the desc method to document your resource type and assist others in understanding what each property and parameter does.

Creating Our Provider

Once we've created our type, we are going to create a simple provider to perform the changes defined in our type on the /etc/shells file. Providers that make use of the ParsedFile class should be stored in a directory named after the type and stored in a file called parsed.rb, for example, /var/puppet/lib/providers/shells/parsed.rb. You can see that provider in Listing 7-8.

Listing 7-8 The /etc/shells Provider

```
require 'puppet/provider/parsedfile'

shells = "/etc/shells"

Puppet::Type.type(:shells).provide(:parsed,
                :parent => Puppet::Provider::ParsedFile,
                :default_target => shells,
                :filetype => :flat
                ) do

                desc "The shells provider that uses the ParsedFile class"

                confine :exists => shells
                text_line :comment, :match => /^#/;
                text_line :blank, :match => /^\s*$/;

                record_line :parsed, :fields => %w{name}
end
```

The first line in Listing 7-8 is a `require` for the `ParsedFile` class we discussed in the type section. The `ParsedFile` is a helper class that can help you manage text-based configuration files. It contains a number of simple functions to parse, edit, and update files. For most of your configuration files, this simple class will probably provide most of the required functionality to manage them.

Tip ➡ I recommend taking a close look at the class contained in the `parsedfile.rb` file located in your `puppet/provider` directory. It has a number of useful features and examples.

Next in Listing 7-8 we've specified the default location of our `/etc/shells` file. We're going to make use of this variable later in our provider.

Then we define the framework for our provider itself. You can see that we've named it `shells`.

We define the `ParsedFile` class as a parent of the provider to enable its functionality and specify some values from the class: the `default_target` value and the file type of the configuration file we're going to manipulate, in our case a flat file. The `default_target` value makes use of the variable we defined earlier with the default location of the `/etc/shells` file. We could override this value by setting the `target` attribute in our resource.

```
target => "/etc/default/shells"
```

We also call `desc` to document our provider.

Next, we specify a `confine` helper method, which tells Puppet to only use the provider if the `/etc/shells` file exists. A number of these helper methods exist to assist in developing and configuring your providers. The `confine` helper method, together with another related helper method, `commands`, determines where the provider is suitable. You can test for a particular file, or a command, using Facter facts or whether a given value is true or false. For example, to make our provider suitable only for a particular operating system, we could use

```
confine :operatingsystem => [:debian, :solaris]
```

The `commands` helper method is similar to a `confine` except that it tells Puppet that a particular binary must be present for the provider to be suitable.

```
commands :yum => "/usr/bin/yum"
```

If you have multiple providers, it is also possible to define a default provider for a particular fact or set of facts. This assists in hiding implementation details from users and allows them to focus on configuring their resource. For example, to declare a provider as the default provider for all Red Hat hosts, you would use the `defaultfor` helper method like so:

```
defaultfor :operatingsystem => :redhat
```

After our helper method, we've defined some functions of the `ParsedFile`. First, we've told Puppet how to identify blank and comment lines in our file using regular expressions. These regular expressions allow `ParsedFile` to process these lines in our file.

Lastly, the `record_line` function is the line that actually adds or removes the shell from the `/etc/shell` file.

```
record_line :parsed, :fields => %w{name}
```

The `ParsedFile` class, combined with the use of the ensurable helper method, tells Puppet that, depending on the setting of the ensure property, a particular shell should be present or absent.

The ensurable helper method also makes three methods available in your providers: `create`, `destroy`, `exists?`. The latter, `exists?`, allows logic to be added that determines whether the particular resource exists. The former methods, `create` and `destroy`, will contain the logic required to either create or destroy the resource, respectively. We're not using these methods as the `ParsedFile` class already provides this functionality, but you could also create a provider that utilized their functionality like so:

```
Puppet::Type.type(:file).provide(:posix) do
    desc "Normal Unix-like POSIX support for file management."

    def create
        File.open(@resource[:name], "w") { |f| f.puts "" } # Create an empty file
    end

    def destroy
        File.unlink(@resource[:name])
    end

    def exists?
        File.exists?(@resource[:name])
    end
end
```

Here we have a provider that makes uses of the three ensureable methods to create, delete, and check for the existence of a file. Using these methods and some simple Ruby, you can perform a variety of useful functions that should allow you to develop basic types.

Back to our `shells` provider; we can see the `record_line` function takes the name of the shell from the `name` variable, in our case, the `shell` parameter in our resource type. In Listing 7-9, you can see an example of a resource that uses our `shells` resource type.

Listing 7-9. A shells *Resource*

```
shells { "/bin/bash":
    ensure => present,
}
```

The resource in Listing 7-9 would add the /bin/bash shell to the /etc/shells file, if it wasn't already present. By changing the `ensure` attribute to `absent`, the resource would remove the shell from the file.

Tip ➡ This is a very simple introduction to constructing providers. To find more about developing providers, refer to the documentation available on the Wiki at
`http://reductivelabs.com/trac/puppet/wiki/ProviderDevelopment`.

Distributing Our New Type

Once we've created our new type and provider, we need to deploy it onto our master servers and clients. The master servers need it to be able to define resources in manifests, and the clients need it to be able to actually implement the resources on the client. To do this distribution, we could install our types and providers into the relevant type and provider directories in the Puppet package. But an easier and more effective method exists that makes use of a Puppet function called `pluginsync`.

The `pluginsync` function synchronizes the contents of a source, called `pluginsource`, to the `libdir` directory. This works in same way `factsync` synchronizes custom facts. The `libdir` directory is defined by default as $vardir/lib, usually /var/puppet/lib. The `pluginsource` option is usually a file mount called `plugins`.

To configure `pluginsync`, we need to configure both our master and client. In Listing 7-10, you can see the required master configuration.

Listing 7-10. The Master pluginsync *Configuration*

```
[main]
pluginsource = puppet://$server/plugins
vardir = /var/puppet
libdir = $vardir/lib
```

In Listing 7-10, we've enabled the pluginsource as the plugins file mount. We've defined vardir to the default location of /var/puppet and finally specified the lib directory, where we will place our custom types and providers on the master. You should place your types in suitable directories. Usually this would be a type and a provider directory, and we would copy our type and provider into the directories. In Listing 7-11, we have created some directories and copied in the custom type and provider we have just created.

Listing 7-11. Creating Our Type and Provider Master Location

```
# mkdir -p /var/puppet/lib/type
# mkdir -p /var/puppet/lib/provider
# mkdir -p /var/puppet/lib/provider/shells
# cp shells.rb /var/puppet/lib/type/shells.rb
# cp parsed.rb /var/puppet/lib/provider/shells/parsed.rb
```

Next, we need to enable this file mount in the fileserver.conf configuration file on our master server as you can see in Listing 7-12.

Listing 7-12. The plugins *Mount*

```
[plugins]
path /var/puppet/lib
allow *.testing.com
```

In Listing 7-12, we've added a plugins mount and allowed access from all testing.com nodes.

Now on our client, we also need to configure pluginsync as you can see in Listing 7-13.

Listing 7-13. Configuring pluginsync *on the Puppet Client*

```
[main]
pluginsync = true
vardir = /var/puppet
libdir = $vardir/lib
pluginsource = puppet://$server/plugins
plugindest = $libdir
```

We enable the `pluginsync` option by setting it to `true`. We then set the `libdir` directory that will be the destination for our custom types and providers. Here we've defined the location as `/var/puppet/lib`. Next, we've specified where Puppet will find custom types, in our case on the `plugins` file mount on our Puppet master. Lastly, we set the `plugindest` option to tell Puppet to place our types and providers in this directory.

After configuration, we restart both the master and the client. When the client next connects to the master, `pluginsync` will be initiated, and our custom types and providers will be downloaded from the file mount into the `/var/lib/puppet/lib` directory.

Tip ➡ You can also ignore some files located in your plug-in source directory; for example, by default any `.svn` directories are ignored, using the `pluginsignore` configuration option.

DISTRIBUTING TYPES AND FACTS IN VERSION 0.24

In the forthcoming 0.24 release of Puppet, an additional distribution mechanism for custom facts and types will also be available. To make use of this method, custom facts and types are now stored in one or more modules. Types and facts associated with particular modules are stored in the associated module. They are then gathered together and distributed via a file server mount called `plugins`. This method has also been previously used in some patched Debian packages released by Matt Palmer.

If your custom facts and types are not specific to particular modules, you can create a catch-all module to distribute them. I recommend calling this module `custom`. To enable the new `pluginsync` functionality, we need to make some changes on both the master and our clients. First we need to configure our `plugins` file mount in the `fileserver.conf` configuration file. If you already have a `plugins` mount, all you need to do is remove the `path` statement from the mount definition. This turns the existing user-defined `plugins` mount into the required system-defined mount. Your resulting mount should look like this:

```
[plugins]
allow *.testing.com
```

Here we've defined the `plugins` mount and allowed clients from the `testing.com` domain to connect and retrieve custom types and facts. Next, we need to create our required module and directory structure. We're going to create the `custom` module to hold our types and facts. We're going to assume our modules directory is `/etc/puppet/modules` (defined using the `modulepath` configuration option).

```
# mkdir -p /etc/puppet/modules/custom/plugins/puppet/type
# mkdir -p /etc/puppet/modules/custom/plugins/facter
```

You place your custom types in the `type` directory and your custom facts in the `facter` directory. If a particular custom type or fact belongs to an already existing module, create the required `plugins/puppet` and `plugins/facter` directories and install your types and facts in them.

Now, on your Puppet clients, you need to configure `pluginsync` and, if you have it enabled, turn off `factsync` as it is no longer needed. You also need to configure the `pluginsource` option to point to the `plugins` mount on the Puppet master server.

```
[main]
pluginsync = true
pluginsource = puppet://$server/plugins
```

You can find some more information on this distribution method at `http://reductivelabs.com/trac/puppet/wiki/PluginsInModules`.

Resources

- *Instructions for adding custom facts:*

  `http://reductivelabs.com/trac/puppet/wiki/AddingFacts`
- *Documentation on how to create custom types:*

  `http://reductivelabs.com/trac/puppet/wiki/CreatingCustomTypes`
- *A complete example of resource type creation:*

  `http://reductivelabs.com/trac/puppet/wiki/CompleteResourceExample`
- *Documentation on detailed provider development:*

  `http://reductivelabs.com/trac/puppet/wiki/ProviderDevelopment`
- *Practical set of documentation covering type development:*

  `http://reductivelabs.com/trac/puppet/wiki/PracticalTypes`

- *Writing your own functions*:

  http://reductivelabs.com/trac/puppet/wiki/WritingYourOwnFunctions

Printed in the United States
107064LV00004BA/15-156/P